THE
BECKETT
ACTOR

THE
BECKETT
ACTOR

Jack MacGowran, Beginning to End

By Jordan R. Young

Foreword by Martin Esslin
Introduction by James Mason

MOONSTONE PRESS

for Tara

THE BECKETT ACTOR
Jack MacGowran, Beginning to End

FIRST EDITION

Published by Moonstone Press
P.O. Box 142, Beverly Hills CA 90213

Frontispiece by Michael O'Reilly
Typeset by Words & Deeds, Los Angeles

Library of Congress Cataloging-in-Publication Data
Young, Jordan R.
    The Beckett actor.
    Bibliography: p.
    Includes index.
    1. MacGowran, Jack, 1918-1973. 2. Actors—Ireland—Biography.
3. Beckett, Samuel, 1906-   —Friends and associates. 4. Beckett, Samuel,
1906-   —Stage history. I. title.
PN 2601.Y68   1987   792'.028'0924 [B]   87-22069
ISBN 0-940410-82-6 (alk. paper)

The paper used in this book complies with the Permanent Paper Standard issued by American National Standards for Information Sciences, ANSI Z39.48-1984.
                    10 9 8 7 6 5 4 3 2 1

Foreword

Jack MacGowran was an extraordinary actor. While he would never have achieved the status of a star like Olivier or Gielgud — his physique and bizarre quality made that impossible — in many ways he could be, and often was, more hauntingly unforgettable than either of these great figures. And he could easily upstage actors of that calibre: simply because there was something unforgettably tragi-comic about his twisted body, his bird-like face and his great piercing eyes.

Samuel Beckett loved Jack MacGowran: if ever there was a perfect congruence between a great poet's imagination and an actor, this was it. There is always a special thrill for a playwright to see the human being he has imagined suddenly leap into concrete, three-dimensional existence. In some ways, and for some of his characters, Jack MacGowran was even better than what Beckett had seen with his mind's eye.

And what is more: with an unerring instinct Jackie found the right intonation, the right gesture, the right tilt of the head for every syllable of text, every second of action Beckett had imagined. It was uncanny to see, when working with Jackie on a Beckett text, how he would render even the most difficult and seemingly obscure turn of phrase crystal-clear and instantly intelligible to anyone listening to him.

I remember producing a reading for BBC Radio of Beckett's poems, in which Jackie tackled that very early, prize-winning effort of Beckett's, *Whoroscope*, a meditation by Descartes on Time, rotten eggs and mortality, a highly baroque and immensely difficult text: miraculously and suddenly, as Jackie's grainy voice spat out the laconic phrases, the situation, the philosopher, and his position at the court of Catherine the Great stood before the mind's eye; all obscurity had disappeared.

Beckett, who is a man of immense humility, is deeply grateful for actors who can miraculously embody his vision with such exactitude and clarity. His relationship to an actress like Billie Whitelaw, an actor like Patrick Magee, was and is based on wonder and awe that there should be human beings so close to his own inner vision.

Jack MacGowran was first among these incarnated embodiments of Beckett's imagined world. There can be no doubt that Jackie became part of his inner vision and inspired Beckett's subsequent work. He truly loved Jack MacGowran, the actor and the man.

Jordan Young's book, meticulously researched, not only preserves a great, unique actor's and artist's life and work for posterity; Jack MacGowran's individual quality and life story also are an essential ingredient in our understanding of the life and work of one of the outstanding creative minds of our time: Samuel Beckett.

Martin Esslin

Rehearsing the one-man show in Dublin, 1971.

Introduction

I saw Jackie MacGowran in a couple of films during the early sixties, including *The Ceremony*, which Laurence Harvey directed. That may have been the first time I saw him perform. I recognized him as an extremely capable actor, but I didn't flip.

The next time I saw him was in Tony Richardson's picture, *Tom Jones*. Now I flipped a little bit more, but not right over the top. I saw that Richardson, like Harvey, was a man of taste and intelligence who recognized a good actor when he saw one.

It was not until I saw Jackie give his one-man performance in his Beckett show at the Lantern Theatre in Dublin in 1965, that he really became what I can loosely describe as my favourite actor. I say "loosely" because every so often one is completely overawed by a new acting talent with which one has, rightly or wrongly, fallen in love. I don't think that anyone has superseded Jackie in my affections and my judgement of actors, although again this must be taken with a grain of salt because Jackie was a marvellous actor in his right context, but was limited to the extent of his physical limitations which would not allow him to play an enormous number of leading parts.

But I cannot think of any live performance on the stage that was better than Jackie's in his Beckett show. Of the few great performances that have impressed me, undoubtedly his was the most outstanding.

What I admire about an actor is that he can completely project himself into the part which he is playing. This does not mean that he has to *live* the part, as people say, because acting is something of a mystery. It is not living, it is make-believe. The sort of acting I am talking about is very closely related to the acting of children when they get together and play make- believe and let's-pretend, and sometimes they are the purest and most perfect actors that you will ever find. Talent and technique, to my mind, have much less importance than this unique gift of being able to pretend in the simple, direct manner of a child.

I can apply this childish simplicity to Jackie MacGowran in connection with every performance I ever saw.

James Mason

Preface

"How can you write about Jackie MacGowran? It's like writing about a butterfly, isn't it?"
— screenwriter Patrick Kirwan

In 1970 I heard about an actor who was performing a one-man show based on the novels, plays and poems of Samuel Beckett. I was intrigued, but skeptical. *Who* was this audacious fellow and how dare he attempt such a thing? How could anyone snip bits and pieces from Beckett and put them on the stage?

I found out when Jack MacGowran toured the U.S. with his show, arriving in Los Angeles for a four-week run. It was winter, and he had an almost hypnotic effect on the opening night audience. His frail, undernourished body fairly crackled with electricity as he moved about the stage; he spoke with such unbridled passion for Beckett's words, and such feeling for them, it was like hearing them for the first time.

Immediately I found myself in MacGowran's debt, and I felt I owed him something. For the moment, I *had* to talk to him. I had to know who he was and where he came from, and how he could do what he did. I had admired and marveled at many performances over the years, but never felt I owed an actor anything beyond the price of admission.

There is something elusive about Jack MacGowran that was difficult to capture on film and is impossible to set down on paper. He radiated this ephemeral quality on stage, and it lives in the memory of all who experienced it. Perhaps this book *is* an attempt to catch a butterfly. But I admire and respect his freedom, and to try and pin that butterfly down or hold him in the hand for more than a moment would be foolish.

Jordan R. Young
Los Angeles
1987

Acknowledgments

My principal debt is to Gloria MacGowran, without whose cooperation and hospitality this biography would have been an even more formidable undertaking. Gloria provided access to precious memorabilia and reluctant interviewees, as well as an abundance of encouragement, candor, patience and constructive criticism over the long evolution of this project; she also reviewed early drafts of the manuscript for accuracy.

Particular thanks are due Jack's stepdaughter, Melanie Carvill, for candid conversation and hospitality in New York; journalist Des Hickey, for making my stay in Dublin so pleasant and productive; the late James Mason, for the letter of tribute that became the introduction to this book; Martin Esslin, for his gracious and lucid foreword; Mel Gussow of *The New York Times*, for allowing me to make use of an unpublished interview; Jack's New York agent, Robert Lantz, for making his prodigious files available; and Dublin photographer Michael O'Reilly, for being so generous with his outstanding work.

I am especially grateful to those friends and associates of Jack MacGowran who took time to share their recollections: Eamonn Andrews, Andrew Anspach, John Beary, Edward Beckett, Denis Brennan, Harry Brogan, E.L. Carew, Bob Casey, Tom Clancy, Michael Clarke-Laurence, May Cluskey, Darach Connolly, Cyril Cusack, Benedict Daly, Rita Darragh, Gordon Davidson, Donal Donnelly, Paddy Dooley, Melvyn Douglas, Hilton Edwards, Gabriel Fallon, Concepta Fennell, Jim Fitzgerald, Brendan Foreman, Eddie Golden, Louis Guss, Gene Gutowski, Mamie Hamilton, Bill Hogarty, Stanley Illsley, Jules Irving, Séamus Kelly, Patrick Kirwan, John Lennon, Mary Lydon, Cathy Lynch, Tomás Mac Anna, Michael McAloney, Danny McCarthy, Kevin McClory, Keith McConnell, Siobhán McKenna, Micheál Mac Liammóir, Donald McWhinnie, Jack Macken, Patrick Magee, Burgess Meredith, Micheál Ó Briain, Eileen O'Casey, Carroll O'Connor, Fred O'Donovan, Maureen O'Hara, Michael O'Herlihy, Brian O'Higgins, Dick O'Rafferty, Grania O'Shannon, Peter O'Toole, Anthony Page, Joseph Papp, Maggie Parker, Donna Pearson, Donald Pleasence, Roman Polanski, Noel Purcell, Godfrey Quigley, Tony Richardson, Paul Scofield, Alan Schneider, Daniel Sheehan, Brendan Smith, Lionel Stander, Dan Sullivan, Sean Treacy, Ronnie Walsh, Billie Whitelaw, Elisabeth Welch and Bud Yorkin.

Additionally I wish to thank the following persons and organizations. In England: Ivan Butler, Eric Ewens, Peter Greenwell, Jocelyn Herbert, Simon Hesera, Moira Lister, Laurence Olivier, Alan Passes, Harold Pinter; Joanna Stephens, Bristol Old Vic; British Broadcasting Company; Gwyniver Jones, BBC Written Archives; Peter Seward, British Film Institute; Leah Schmidt, Curtis Brown Group; National Film Archive; Paramount House; Jacqui French, Thames TV. In France: Peter Brook, Eugène Ionesco, Nina Soufy.

In Ireland: Beatrice Behan, Ursula Doyle, Bill Foley, Carmel Mallaghan, Anna Manahan, Wolf Mankowitz, Angela Moloney, Alec Reid, Gerard Victory; Mairin Woods, Abbey Theatre; Actor's Equity; Patricia Turner, Dublin Gate Theatre; Joe Kearns, Gaiety Theatre; *The Irish Independent; The Irish Press; The Irish Times;* Barbara Durack, Radio Telefís Éireann.

In the United States: Bert Andrews, Dick Bann, Winfred Blevins, Richard Brockway, Richard Brooks, Hector Caballero, John Calder, Gary Claussen, Ruby Cohn, Nancy Dragoun, Lucy Dutton, Chester Erskine, Charles FitzSimons, Bill Heckman, Malcolm Hill, Winton C. Hoch, Florence Johnson, Bert Kolker, Rosette Lamont, Liam Lenihan, Leo Leyden, Alma Lynch, Sean McClory, Betty Miller, Arthur and Estelle Nitikman, Dan O'Herlihy, Dick Nash, Carla Rosenquist, Kathryn Ryan, Sandra Schmidt, Joseph Siegman, Valerie Sowder, Robert Symonds, Richard Toscan, Pam Young, Philip and Pearl Young.

Also in the U.S.: Academy of Motion Picture Arts and Sciences; Eddie Brandt's Saturday Matinee; California State University, Fullerton; Cinemabilia; Columbia Pictures; Larry Edmunds Book Shop; KCET Public Television, Los Angeles; Metro-Goldwyn-Mayer; Movie Star News; New York Public Library at Lincoln Center; Lynn Holst, New York Shakespeare Festival; Tina Howe, Special Collections, Northwestern University Library; Jerry Ohlinger's Movie Material Store; Republic Pictures; Harry Ransom Humanities Research Center, University of Texas at Austin; United Artists; University of California, Los Angeles; University of Southern California; Walt Disney Productions; Warner Brothers; and Mr. Krapp, for the use of his tape recorder.

Finally, I am indebted to Jack MacGowran himself, for making time for an unabashed admirer when he had so little time left; to Samuel Beckett, for kind permission to quote from his work, and from his letters to MacGowran; and both for providing the inspiration that was the driving force behind this book.

Photo by Michael O'Reilly

Prologue

Jack MacGowran had a fear of life and a fear of death he could not shake. From the outset of his career, he was terrified of going on stage. His depressions and stage fright grew worse when he stopped drinking; he had an absolute panic he could no longer submerge in alcohol.

But he lived only to perform, and he gave himself to it at the sacrifice of everything else. If he was too tired to go on towards the end, he denied it. He had struggled too long and labored too hard, he had come too far to yield to defeat.

The year before his death he embarked upon an arduous tour of one-night stands, an ill-planned schedule he could barely endure. Yet he felt an obligation to Samuel Beckett and, moreover, to his public. Those hungry young minds, eager to listen and open to swallow his and Beckett's vision of the human predicament, he couldn't let them down.

One day in Philadelphia he suffered through the matinee, in need of dental surgery. Before the evening performance his wife took him to the hospital. Anaesthetic was out of the question. He simply had to go on that night; his one-man show, adapted from the works of Beckett, had sold out the house.

The actor was prepared and looking forward to the show when he returned — until the theatre manager saw him. "You look awful," said the manager. "You can't go on." If anyone told him he looked awful, he *looked* awful. His wife, Gloria, had gone to get some pain-killer. When she walked into the foyer of the Annenberg Center, she heard people stirring. "MacGowran's had surgery," said someone. "He can't go on."

She rushed back to the dressing room. "What's going on?" she said calmly. "I'm not going on," said Jack. "They said I look awful. I feel awful." Gloria turned on the intercom so he could hear the audience arriving. Jack started to perk up. Gloria began talking to him, and he started to relax.

"It seems a terrible pity not to go on," she said. Jack had to agree. He began to put on his makeup. The theatre manager was afraid to let him go on, in case something happened in his theatre. But MacGowran was determined; if he let the audience down, it would worry him for months. He might be too depressed to continue the tour.

Gloria pushed him on, then took her seat out front. She waited with uncertainty as the house grew dark.

A faint glimmer of light touched the stage. A harsh, barren landscape began to take shape as the light grew bright, then brighter. The cast of one failed to appear. Gloria began to squirm in her seat. *Where is he? What's happened to him?*

At last he trudged on, his stick-like body hunched forward, shrouded in the large black greatcoat he wore with humble pride. Head bowed, shoulders drooping, he took a few hesitant steps, his bare ankles peeking above his dilapidated boots. He stopped and looked about, his rheumy eyes surveying the landscape, his ravaged face devoid of all emotion.

There was absolute quiet. The decrepit little man stood and stared into the void without saying a word. *Oh, my God,* thought Gloria. *What have I done?* And then, after the longest moment, he began to speak, ever so slowly, ejaculating the words from his toothless skull in a plain, coarse voice of utter conviction.

> I shall soon be quite dead at last in spite of all. Perhaps next month. Then it will be the month of April or of May. For the year is still young, a thousand little signs tell me so...

The audience sat rapt, motionless. They began to giggle uncomfortably as the old man continued to assert his demise, with a glint of satisfaction in his eye.

> I could die today, if I wished, merely by making a little effort, if I could wish, if I could make an effort. But it is just as well to let myself die, quietly, without rushing things...

Unable to stifle their laughter, in the face of his grim pronouncement, the audience roared uncontrollably, as Beckett's laconic shards of language danced from the actor's lips.

> Yes, I shall be natural at last, I shall suffer more, then less, without drawing any conclusions, I shall pay less heed to myself, I shall be neither hot nor cold any more, I shall be... tepid, I shall die tepid, without enthusiasm. I shall not watch myself die, that would spoil everything. Have I watched myself live? Have I ever complained? Then why rejoice now? I am content, necessarily, but not to the point of clapping my hands...

For the next two hours MacGowran stood and sat and tramped about the stage in that tattered, ankle-length coat, rasping, cackling,

Photo by Michael O'Reilly

roaring, keening, his voice rich with the poetry and the pain, the humor and the horror of Beckett's universe. The convoluted gibberish that had teased and tormented two generations of scholars — and intimidated all but a handful of actors — tumbled from his tongue as clear and crisp and uncomplicated as a series of nursery rhymes, with all its linguistic foreplay and brooding humor intact.

"I think Jack gave the most brilliant performance of his life that night," said Gloria MacGowran in retrospect. "He had me frozen in my seat — and he knew *exactly* what he was doing. Afterwards he said, 'I knew I could do it, but I had a captive audience.'"

Jack MacGowran had a stage presence that was the envy of actors throughout the world. From the moment he made his entrance, before he ever opened his mouth, his audience was completely in sympathy with him. They knew where he was coming from and where he was going without a word being uttered. When he stepped on stage he came alive, channeling a day's energies into an evening's performance; he held the attention like a magnetic force.

One night in Washington, D.C., there was an unexpected confrontation. MacGowran was nearing the very end of his show, a delicate and quiet moment. Suddenly, a drunk in the balcony began to laugh. The disturbance was too loud to ignore; it threatened to destroy the actor's bond with his audience. A line from Beckett's *Endgame* leaped to mind, as MacGowran fixed his gaze on the man and shouted to the balcony:

Well, there's nothing funnier than unhappiness, I grant you that.

The laughter stopped cold, and the audience was his once more.

In the beginning, as in the end, MacGowran had always to go his own way. He wanted success, but he wanted it on his own terms, and he could not abide by anyone else's limitations. He migrated from Dublin to Paris to London to New York seeking something he couldn't find in his native Ireland, but he never forgot where he came from.

The obstacles in his path were many and not easily overcome. He was hindered at the outset by his working class background; he was further handicapped by his small stature and unusual appearance. Years passed before he transcended the stereotype of the Stage Irishman and made his uniqueness work to his advantage, in the plays of Sean O'Casey and the films of Roman Polanski.

The role that eventually made a name for him throughout the world was a part he was better equipped to play than any other actor. He was intimately acquainted not only with Samuel Beckett, but with the characters that peopled the author's novels and plays; he identified

Photo by Michael O'Reilly

with their dark souls in a way no one else could. He recognized Hamm and Clov's black Irish humor because he had grown up with it; he knew Molloy's hopelessness because he had lived it. He played their desperation from the inside out.

But he also sensed the affirmation of life at the core of Beckett's work that had eluded others. Where critics and scholars stressed the nihilism and the despair, MacGowran was aroused by the writer's wit and compassion. The actor had changed people's minds about Shaw and illuminated the darkest corners of O'Neill, and he sought to alter the public's perception of Beckett. With the author's supervision, he took selections from the novels and plays and wove them together, to reveal the humanity and the joy that he knew to be at the center of a most misunderstood and private man.

The result was Beckett distilled to his essence, a lone figure on an empty stage, his only prop a ragged handkerchief, his chair a jagged rock. The show was a triumph in Dublin, a sensation in Paris, a phenomenon in New York. At the Schiller-Theater Workshop in Berlin, it caused a furor, a commotion of the sort generally reserved for pop stars.

Beifallssturm für ein überwältigendes Solo: Jack MacGowran

A storm of applause for an overpowering performance, said the headline in the *Berliner Zeitung*. A *Sturm* of such fury it took 12 curtain calls to abate, 12 only because MacGowran was physically unable to take more — to the anger of his fans. When Schiller dramaturg Albert Bessler asked Beckett for permission to do the show with a German actor, he was refused. "I don't want anyone else to do it except Jack," said Sam. "No one else *could* do it but Jack."

MacGowran could hold an audience in the palm of his hand, but he couldn't cope with life; his was a melancholy existence made bearable only by his love of acting. In the end, he was no longer an actor playing a part but a man lost in the bowels of a character. The words were Beckett's, but the pain — and the torment — were his.

> ...where I am, I don't know, I'll never know, in the silence you don't know, you must go on, I can't go on, I'll go on.

1

His mother wanted a son who looked like Leslie Howard, and she never let him forget it. Jack MacGowran could never live up to her lofty expectations, much less his own. As a boy, he yearned to be a brain surgeon, an athlete, a writer; he felt he had to make his mark in the world. But as a young man seeking direction in life he did not aspire to excellence; only as an actor did he pursue his endeavors with every fiber of his being. He was limited less by his own abilities than by the constraints imposed on him by others. The words of a fellow Irishman, a dozen years his senior, would ultimately liberate him from those restrictions.

"I was born when I met Sam Beckett," he observed toward the end of his life. "So I've had two existences on this sphere. In the attempt to run away from myself I ran into myself."

This confrontation he compared with the experience of sailing from California, after making a Walt Disney film, consuming an inexhaustible supply of vodka on the voyage to Southampton. Instead of having a hangover on reaching England, MacGowran found himself "just divided into two people in the way you might see two images of a person through a camera, but I could not bring them into focus to make a complete whole.

"Perhaps these were the two people I was made of," he agonized. "Not fucking even formed into one being after the age of thirty. How many real areas are there in the mind and how many were closed to finally open and Christ help us how many more will open?"

John Joseph McGowran began the first of those two existences on October 13, 1918, in a two-story red brick house on the south side of Dublin. He lived with his family in Ranelagh, a few short miles from where Samuel Beckett had grown up in the Dublin suburb of Foxrock.

World War I came to an end a few short weeks after he was born, but Ireland itself was in the throes of revolution. As a child, Johnny McGowran (he later changed the spelling) was far too young to understand the significance of the Anglo-Irish War, and the War of Independence that followed. But he knew the gunshots being fired in Dublin streets — and the explosions that rocked the city — were not the sounds of boys playing soldier. Nor were the Black and Tans professional soldiers; they were convicts recruited from English prisons, and promised their freedom if they would help quell the rebellion.

The war-ravaged streets of Dublin were none too safe for civilians, but the violence was fairly centralized. Jack's mother was wheeling him in a pram one day when a Black and Tans walked up in his mismatching khaki and black leather uniform, and jokingly pointed a gun in the child's face; it was the boy's only brush with The Troubles so vividly depicted by Sean O'Casey in his early plays.

Try as he might to declare his independence, Jack was to call 46 Lower Beechwood Avenue home until he was in his mid-thirties. His Dublin-born, working class parents couldn't understand why he wanted so desperately to leave the nest. Matthew and Gertrude McGowran had, after all, given their only son a wholesome Catholic upbringing and a proper education; upon graduation they secured for him what they considered "a good, safe job" — a position in an insurance company.

Matthew J. McGowran eked out a living as a *commercial traveller*, a traveling salesman who drove the narrow back roads of rural Ireland. On a rare visit to the theatre in his later years, he went to see his son in *Death of a Salesman*; tears came to his eyes when he saw himself in Willy Loman's well-worn shoes.

The elder McGowran, who lost his job consistently, had a tendency to lose his temper with even greater frequency. Violent displays of anger were not uncommon; the slightest difference of opinion between father and son could lead to a loud and angry row. A quiet, gentle child, Jack grew increasingly determined not to lose his temper. As he got older, he kept things bottled up inside, things that wanted a release.

With his father on the road he was the man of the house. But in a house inundated with women — his mother, his sisters Mamie and Rita, his aunt and her daughter — he never learned to assert himself. When World War II broke out the young man made a futile effort to break away by volunteering for the RAF, but they rejected him. Or so he thought. Weeks later, he learned his mother had intervened by tearing up the acceptance papers.

Jack was a voracious reader. He spent much of his youth with his nose buried in a book, in his room upstairs at the back of the house. He also enjoyed writing poetry, which became a means of getting attention from a father who had little time for him, as much as a form of self-expression. His father was so proud of a poem about the Shamrock Rovers football team, he had it printed in leaflets and distributed. But Jack's friends always requested the one about going for a ride on a tandem bike, with a girl whose bloomers got caught in the wheels.

It was in Tommy O'Rourke's class at the Christian Brothers School in Synge Street that Jack got his first exposure to literature, memorizing Anglo-Irish verse and studying Shakespeare. O'Rourke was a brash character whose English and history lessons made a formidable impression in young minds; he imbued his students with a love of poetry he could not supress.

O'Rourke planted in MacGowran an affection for the dramatic and literary arts that grew fast and furiously. The seeds of a curiosity were sown too, something that wanted more than what was on the printed page — a hunger to know who and what and why a writer was — how he conceived ideas and put words together, and everything inbetween.

MacGowran's own attempts at writing succeeded only in frustrating him, but the hunger did not abate. His unrelenting curiosity would manifest itself years later, as he sought out writers themselves — Jack Yeats, Sean O'Casey, Eugène Ionesco, and most fruitfully Samuel Beckett. The keener his knowledge of the man, the actor reasoned, the sharper his interpretation of their work.

According to his classmates, young Johnny McGowran did little to call attention to himself in school. He was an average student who took a light- hearted approach to his studies. He and his best friend offset the drudgery of homework by doing their lessons together with another classmate, on a billiard table between games of snooker. Each of them specialized in a subject, with Jack excelling in English. He was no mean snooker player either.

MacGowran was often truant from school as a boy, sneaking into the neighborhood movie house whenever he could. The fact that movies were often years old by the time they reached Ireland — and badly truncated as well — did nothing to diminish their lure. For two pence he could spend the afternoon with his celluloid heroes, enchanted by the acrobatic antics of Harold Lloyd and Buster Keaton, the smooth moves of Fred Astaire and Ginger Rogers, and the cool, sure-footed arrogance of Jimmy Cagney.

Jack was not the only dreamer in the "No-Pass Class" of 1936. Cornelius Ryan, who would later write *The Longest Day*, and Liam Cosgrave, who became Prime Minister of Ireland, were among the 40 students who took their Leaving Certificate from Christian Brothers that year. Like Jack, their minds were on something decidedly beyond their lessons; they were far too preoccupied with the future to concentrate on the present.

Matthew McGowran could not afford to send his only son to the university, where Jack might continue his studies and realize his ambition to become a surgeon. Upon graduation Jack took a correspondence course and entered the employ of the Hibernian Insurance Company, where he inspected claims and drafted policies in the fire department.

While he proved a conscientious worker, he sought every possible diversion off the job. He served as an assistant scoutmaster and performed comic monologues in Boy Scout variety shows; he also sang in dance halls with a band called the Red Tigers, recited poetry and did mimicry at parties.

If he had a gift for entertaining people, he was scarcely aware of it in those days. "Johnny was modest and unassuming. He wasn't a personality," recalled a former schoolmate. "You didn't know he was there until he was called upon to perform."

The activity that took precedence over everything in Jack's busy life at this time was athletics — a passion he shared with Samuel Beckett. Where young Beckett had left his mark on Dublin's cricket fields, MacGowran excelled in the high jump. Jack was runner-up in the National Championship at one point, but he slowed his progress by experimenting with different styles and never achieved his full potential.

"Johnny never worked hard enough on technique to perfect his jumping," observed high jump champion Dick O'Rafferty, his constant competitor and drinking companion in those days. "He wouldn't allow technique to make a machine out of him; he had to express himself in his own way. Johnny would come as near as dammit to beating me, but never quite. He did a bit of training on occasion but it was harmless; he was at his best when he did no training at all."

During World War II MacGowran and O'Rafferty were asked to go to County Kildare for a track and field exhibition in Kilcullen. They were instructed to take a bus to the village of Ballymore Eustace, where they would be collected. The boys started off at dawn, still suffering from hangovers they had earned the night before. Upon their arrival in the village they bumped into the local parish priest, who suspected they had left Dublin rather early.

"Naturally, he yanked us into mass," said O'Rafferty. "If he'd left us inside the door, we might've sat on our rucksacks and fallen asleep, but there wasn't a spare inch in the church — except right up at the altar. It was the longest mass, it went on and on; it was interminable. It nearly cured us forever." Unfortunately, it did nothing of the kind.

Despite the occasional hangover, Johnny McGowran was a clean-living boy and not one to shirk his religious duties. Weekly attendance at church was mandatory, but there were compensations; his father was as religious about the Sunday match as he was about Sunday mass.

In addition to football games and polo matches, the children were also taken to see old-fashioned variety shows, particularly the English music hall performers their father was so fond of, whenever they came to town. Jack would never forget his first visit to the theatre — the majestic Gaiety in South King Street — as long as he lived.

A packed house buzzed with anticipation as the magnificent yellow and gold brocade curtain rose. Young Johnny sat spellbound in his plush red seat as Jimmy O'Dea, the 5 foot-4 inch clown prince of Ireland, entered to the accompaniment of his familiar theme.

The audience roared with delight as their beloved Jimmy, adorned in dark wig and rusted skirt, replete with apron, shawl and petticoat, became Biddy Mulligan of the caustic wit and razor-edged tongue. Jack would later remember him as "my earliest and most profound influence."

MacGowran and his sisters sometimes put on their own shows in a neighbor's garage. Among their neighbors and childhood playmates was Maureen O'Hara, née FitzSimons, who "went Hollywood" at 14. Jack's career did not develop beyond the garage-show phase until his sister, Mamie, joined the Rathmines and Rathgar Musical Society. One night, as a joke, she suggested to her younger brother that he attend a meeting. Jack took her seriously, and immediately found the group's activities to his liking.

MacGowran was 22 when he made his debut with Rathmines and Rathgar at the Gaiety Theatre in November 1940, singing in the chorus of three Gilbert and Sullivan operettas. Time-honored frivolities like *The Pirates of Penzance* and *Trial by Jury* not only provided him with his first stage experience, but introduced him to songs that would remain favorites, reliable for a turn at party or pub.

When the group went into rehearsal for *The Student Prince* in 1943, a young man was selected from the chorus for the role of Nicholas, the flautist; when he decided he didn't want to leave the chorus, Jack was chosen in his place. He too was apprehensive, but he was persuaded to take the part.

That fall, when a member of Rathmines and Rathgar was called to read for an outside show, he brought MacGowran along for moral support. The shy, spindly young man with the prominent nose and protruding teeth, elastic neck and bulging Adam's apple, made a highly favorable impression on producer-playwright Brendan Smith.

As a result of the audition, Jack won a leading role in *You Are Invited*; his companion failed to make the cast. MacGowran's performance in this farce at the Peacock Theatre — as a young man whose mother tries to launch him on an acting career by giving parties in theatrical circles — was prophetic. It not only launched him on his own acting career but initiated a fruitful association with Smith and a lasting romance with Dublin drama critics.

"I was immediately struck by Jack's appearance," recalled Smith. "In the plays and revues that followed, I found I was writing parts, mainly lead comedy roles, especially for him. It started with his appearance and then went into the deeper area of his interpretative talents. I would pick up on particular characteristics — for instance, the cadence of his speech — and write these spontaneously into the dialogue."

On his second outing with Smith, as a bookworm in *One Man's Heaven, The Irish Press* enthused, "McGowran's comedy acting ran away with the whole play." Jack also scored in the title role of A.A. Milne's *Mr. Pim Passes By*, a sentimental part with an element of pathos that was well-suited to his talents.

In 1945 actor and producer presented the revue *A Spring Cocktail* — in which Jack did a parody of Fred Astaire — as a Brendan Smith-Jack MacGowran production. Despite the fanfare, it was a essentially a publicity gimmick.

> A new and interesting partnership has been announced in Dublin theatreland. It is that of Brendan Smith, author-producer-actor, and Jack McGowran, whose comedy work has been such a conspicuous feature of Brendan Smith productions over the last two years... McGowran is an actor who is at his best in comedy, getting his effects with effortless ease and having that unusual quality of raising laughs without opening his mouth.
> — *The Evening Mail*, April 23, 1945

MacGowran changed the spelling of his surname from "Mc" to "Mac" at this time. It was to be misspelled often through his career.

Concurrent with his work in Smith's company Jack formed his own group, The Utopians, putting on shows at a local tennis club. One of the group's more unusual presentations was a short play MacGowran wrote himself, in which he fell asleep in a rehearsal room and dreamt he traveled through time.

Jack was also active in the Pilgrim Players at this time, under the direction of Julie Hamilton, appearing in plays like *Gaslight* and *Hobson's Choice*. He appeared in presentations staged by the Boy Scouts and took part in the Hilton Edwards-Micheál Mac Liammóir production of *Abraham Lincoln*.

During the run of John Drinkwater's *Lincoln* at the Dublin Gate Theatre, there was an outbreak of influenza. As illness wrought havoc

Rehearsing in Dublin with actress Aileen Harte.

with the cast, Edwards found himself in trouble, with few understudies to fall back on.

"Somebody would go down with the flu and I thought, 'What the hell are we going to do?' And Jackie would say, 'I can play that part tonight.' He played practically every part except Mrs. Lincoln, very rapidly and very brilliantly — and literally saved our bacon for that," acknowledged Edwards.

Brendan Smith's semi-professional company put their shows on in whatever theatres were available, most frequently the 102-seat Peacock adjacent to the Abbey Theatre. The plays were done on a profit-sharing basis, and gradually the actors were paid. But Smith's abilities as a dramatist were limited — by his own admission — and shows sometimes went into rehearsal with only the first act written.

MacGowran's acting often made up for the deficiencies of the script. "Jack was so responsive to my direction, so quick to seize on the essential element in the make-up of a character," said Smith, who went on to become director of the Dublin Theatre Festival. "An actor in the course of a play has time to put over only so many characteristics, and Jack was quite brilliant in being able to select the essentials, develop them and get them across to an audience."

Gabriel Fallon, *The Evening Standard's* eminent theatre critic, ventured backstage one night at the Peacock to see one of the actors — "MacGowran, or whatever his name was. I met him and asked if he was interested in the theatre," remembered Fallon. "He said he was. Then I asked him the second question I always asked young actors in those days — did he have a regular job? He said he did. I usually told them to stick to their job. But I told Jackie, 'If I had the money I'd put it behind you and make a fortune for both of us.'

"I thought of Jackie as a potential Chaplin. He had the same quality as Chaplin, in that once you saw him you never forgot him," said Fallon. When MacGowran asked the critic — a former Abbey actor — if he would use his influence to get Jack into the National Theatre, Fallon tried to discourage him. "I didn't think the Abbey was the right place for Jackie. It didn't tally with what I saw in him; he wasn't their type," observed Fallon. "But he was very keen on the Abbey — he was determined to get in."

Jack's superiors at the Hibernian Insurance Company were beginning to take a dim view of his after-hours activities. To pacify his employers, he adopted the stage name of Grene Hanning — the protagonist of a novel he was reading about a devout Catholic who left the church.

By this time he and Brendan Smith had had a falling out, bringing to an end their happy and prolific collaboration. Jack played a summer season with Stanley Illsley and Leo McCabe, then joined them at the Olympia Theatre in the fall of 1946. His nom de théâtre did not disguise him from the critics, who singled him out for his performances in J.B. Priestley's *When We Are Married* and *While the Sun Shines*.

"Jackie had a wonderful flair for comedy even in those days. He had a natural sense of timing and a wonderful face," said Illsley. "He could be funny without mugging. If you want to learn anything about the theatre, you've got to do it the hard way — and Jackie did."

As Hanning, Jack also made his directorial debut at this time, piloting *Ladies in Retirement* for the Pilgrim Players. *The Irish Independent* remarked that MacGowran's acting in the play as well was a mistake, "as apparently it meant that he never sat out front and saw the production as a whole." A rival newspaper disagreed:

> Grene Hanning's Albert Feather, a brilliant Cockney character study — half comic-half sinister — shines even among the first-rate performances of the rest of the cast.
> — *The Irish Times*, October 16, 1946

While he toiled away the daytime hours as an insurance clerk, by night MacGowran was making a name for himself as one of the most popular young actors in town. Though he was earning £8 a week at the Hibernian — more than double what the Abbey Theatre could pay him — the call of the footlights grew overwhelming.

Co-worker Eamonn Andrews, who subsequently quit the Hibernian to devote full time to his job as a radio announcer, recalled the decisive moment. "Johnny was taking a bigger jump than I was by leaving the company, but he was set on going into the theatre. He knew they wouldn't approve at home, but he was not going to be stopped," said Andrews. "He was gone into his own world."

Jack told his mother he couldn't see himself sitting at a desk and pushing a pen for the rest of his life. It was not an impulsive move — he had pondered leaving the job for more than two years. His involvement in amateur theatrics was on the upswing; his inner yearnings, to say nothing of the praise he was drawing from the critics and the public, could no longer be ignored.

The approval of others was of no little importance to MacGowran, and he continually sought assurance from those around him. He met *Irish Times* columnist Séamus Kelly after a Pilgrim production and asked what his professional prospects were.

"I told him he'd probably be crucified for a long time, but that he'd make it if he could stick out the hard times," remembered Kelly. "I thought he'd make the grade — he had that great quality the French call *droll*."

The second annual Abbey Christmas pantomime was being cast late in 1946 when one of the junior members of the company — who had seen him in some of Brendan Smith's productions — suggested they cast Jack in the role of a leprechaun.

Fernando and the Dragon also featured a young redhead, who played a girl from the bog and wore a purple dress with a long slit up the side. The managing director of the Abbey warned her repeatedly to sew up the dress, and to stop making jokes about the President of Ireland. Siobhán McKenna simply ignored him.

"Neither MacGowran's blas nor greasepaint could hide the

identity of an up-and-coming comedian," wrote Gabriel Fallon of Jack's first Abbey performance. "Two years from now — if not sooner — everyone will be claiming to have first discovered him."

One of his earliest boosters, Fallon two years later declared:

> Every time I see this lad on the stage I wish I had the money to pay, train and present to the world an Irish droll, who, given the opportunity, would make even Chaplin a fading memory.
> — *The Evening Standard*, January 1949

2

As World War II came to an end, Dublin's Abbey Theatre neared the conclusion of its Golden Era. The great playwrights, on whose work the theatre had built its illustrious name, had passed away or gone into artistic exile. The actors who had brought to life the immortal characters of Yeats and O'Casey and Synge and Shaw in the first productions of those plays — actors like Barry Fitzgerald and Sara Allgood and Arthur Shields — had met an even more lamentable fate. They were in Hollywood making movies.

Thus it fell upon the legendary F.J. McCormick, the most gifted of the lot, to uphold the Abbey's international reputation. He too was beckoned with the promise of movie stardom, but he was not to be persuaded; his loyalty was to the Abbey.

McCormick had acted every conceivable role from Oedipus and Lear to O'Casey's Joxer Daly; neither the flimsy kitchen comedies in which he was sometimes cast, nor the meager salary he received, could dissuade him from his devotion to the theatre. He was a guiding light to the younger members of the company and an inspiration to all. He embodied the very essence of the actor's craft, particularly to one young aspirant.

Drafting insurance policies, respectable as it may have been, was a job in which MacGowran saw no future. The Abbey Theatre, where he was appearing in the Christmas pantomime, held a hope for him and a promise. His allegiance was to the theatre, not the Hibernian; when instructed to settle claims out of court, he often advised the claimant to hold out for more money.

His theatrical ambitions waiting in the wings, MacGowran soldiered through the winter of 1946-47, biding his time until the opportunity presented itself to make a dramatic exit. On a cold February day Jack went for his fellowship examination at the Chartered Insurance Institute in Abbey Street. Taking the advancement exam was pointless, but he had to take it — and pass it — for his own satisfaction.

Jack completed his paper a few minutes before the end of the allotted hour. As he started to fold up his paper, he knocked over a bottle of ink, spilling it on everything; he tore the paper up in a rage, left the mess as it was and walked out.

He later asserted that something in his subconscious had caused him to knock the bottle over. In any case, he could wish for no better excuse to cross the road and apply for a job at the drab, L-shaped building that housed the Abbey Players — "an L of a place," the locals called it.

The National Theatre had enough able character actors in its employ at the moment, however, and managing director Ernest Blythe told MacGowran he had room for no more. In desperation, Jack sat outside the director's office, determined to "wear the man down." But when at last Blythe relented and hired him, MacGowran found the Abbey indeed had all the eager young players it could use — as well as the more seasoned performers, who won the choice assignments.

In March, a cast list was posted on the bulletin board for *The Dark Road*, a new play by Elizabeth Connor. Abbey veterans Harry Brogan and May Craig were given the leading roles, while MacGowran had to content himself with the small part of a doctor.

Jack came home from rehearsal with tears in his eyes the night of April 24. "F.J. is dead," he cried aloud. Death had taken the 56-year-old McCormick at the pinnacle of his career. *Odd Man Out*, one of his rare excursions into films, had just been released; New York newspapers were raving about his extraordinary performance on the very day of his passing.

It was a heartfelt loss to the Abbey Theatre and a shattering blow to Jack. McCormick himself had turned his back on a comfortable job as a civil servant — against his parents' wishes — and MacGowran no doubt identified with him. The young hopeful and his idol, who had inspired him to join the Abbey, would never have the chance to work together.

Jack made his debut as a member of the company on May 12, 1947. His real initiation into the theatre, however, was to come a few nights later when he and Harry Brogan had to drag a corpse offstage, and got their signals crossed. Each of them grabbed a leg and walked off on opposite sides of a canvas wall.

"Back up," whispered Brogan. "Back up." They retraced their steps and dragged the body off, then propped the dummy in a rocking chair and left it in the wings — a toy cigarette with a glowing red tip dangling at its crotch — to greet their fellow actors.

Like the other members of the company, Jack was billed under his Irish name, Séan Mac Shamhráin. He was not long in their midst, however, when the older members affectionately dubbed him "The Snitch," in reference to his nose. But MacGowran did not have to be reminded of his extraordinary features; he had only to look in a mirror to realize he would never play Hamlet.

Abbey actor F.J. McCormick, right, as Shell in *Odd Man Out* with James Mason.

It was not so much the size of Jack's proboscis that stood in the way of fulfillment at the Abbey, as the narrow-mindedness of producers like Michael J. Dolan, who did not look upon him with great favor. The unique qualities that Samuel Beckett and Roman Polanski would later make the most of worked against Jack from his earliest professional days.

With little demand for his talents at the Abbey, "Snitchy" kept busy by directing productions for a variety of amateur dramatic groups in Dublin and the neighboring provinces. Fellow Abbey actors sometimes joined the cast of his shows as a lark.

An avid reader, MacGowran did not confine himself to the literature of the theatre. He developed an interest in figures as diverse as Gandhi and Nijinsky and eagerly absorbed himself in the study of their lives. His fascination with Nijinsky moved him to spend a considerable amount of time at the Abbey School of Ballet, where he reportedly took lessons in the art.

He also studied a young dancing student. They fell in love and decided to get married, but her parents and his salary intervened. The diminutive actor who was ten years her senior — and took home a weekly pay of £3 and 10 shillings — did not impress his prospective in-laws as the ideal match for their daughter.

Jack announced his engagement to a number of young women in the next few years, though none managed to bring him to the altar. "Getting engaged was nothing unusual for him," affirmed former Abbey actress Grania O'Shannon, one of many fiancées. "I guess he thought it was the honorable thing to do."

MacGowran would do anything to keep a relationship going, but little to develop one; he was comfortable enough with women, but he didn't want the responsibility. When Jack's mother asked if he would marry and settle down, he replied that he was married to the theatre — which, he declared, would remain his mistress and his only love.

It was a one-sided romance, as far as the Abbey Theatre was concerned. Managing director Ernest Blythe, a former Minister for Finance who had engineered an all-important government subsidy for the Abbey, was a figure of total and unbending authority. Politics and economics were his metier, not art and aesthetics. He insisted that Abbey actors be fluent in the Irish language and expected them to speak it with Northern inflections, as he did; he failed to cast MacGowran in a number of productions on the excuse that his Irish was insufficient.

Try as they might to improve their lot, young actors found the situation hopeless. "Jack and I felt the Abbey should do O'Neill," said actor Ronnie Walsh. "We suggested this to Blythe several times, but he dismissed Eugene O'Neill as not being in the Abbey tradition.

"Jack was greatly frustrated in those days. He felt nobody would get anywhere as long as Blythe was around. We would often walk home together, plotting how to get rid of the man — short of summary execution."

Blythe knew little about the theatre, but he knew enough to have his opinions about it. He felt that actors didn't need money, and told them it wasn't good for them. The younger members of the company all lived at home with their parents, which was as good an excuse as any for not giving them a raise — but then, Blythe used any excuse when it came to money.

Young Abbey players were not to be restrained by a lack of funds. "Many times Jack was broke, like the rest of us," recalled Micheál

Ó Briain, who shared a dressing room with him. "As long as you had your entrance fee into a bar, you were elected; all you needed was the price of a pint, and you could borrow that. Jackie and I would have five or six pints and then walk home."

The actors were a hard-working lot, but their labors never interfered with their fun. There was often a poker game going in the theatre wings, and parties were sometimes held on the stage after a show. Between morning and evening performances they were usually to be found engaging in their favorite sport, in Barney O'Beirne's Liffey Bar or Vincent Timmons' pub in Townsend Street.

Two doors down from the Liffey Bar on Eden Quay, around the corner from the Abbey, was a small tobacco shop they patronized daily. Paddy Dooley, the amiable proprietor, was a round little man with an unusual affinity for theatre people. He was a fixture at opening nights and, in his own special way, a patron of the arts. He looked after the actors and hoarded cigarettes — a precious post-war commodity — for them; he lent them money and let them "put it on the slate."

The Quays tobacconist remembered MacGowran in later years with a warmth and affection uncharacteristic of Dublin. "Jackie always had a smile on his face when he came in. He made you feel like you were the only person he knew. He was a great listener — he could stand there and listen to you talk for hours," said Dooley. "Very seldom would you see him in a bad humor. No matter what trouble you had, Jackie would minimize it down to a small thing."

The storied Abbey Theatre, its intimate little stage scarcely bigger than Dooley's storefront, was Mecca to MacGowran. But the parts he managed to obtain during his three-year stay were few. Among them were the role of a farmer in John Millington Synge's *The Playboy of the Western World*, a desperado in *The Shewing Up of Blanco Posnet* by Bernard Shaw, and a walk-on as a man who wants to buy some poison in Lennox Robinson's *Drama at Inish*.

MacGowran saw the chance he had been waiting for when M.J. Dolan announced a revival of Sean O'Casey's *The Plough and the Stars*, which had caused riots when it premièred at the Abbey in 1926. Yearning to play O'Casey and brimming with enthusiasm, Jack voiced his desire for the part of the explosive Young Covey. It was a bitter disappointment when a fellow actor was awarded the role.

The annual Christmas pantomimes gave MacGowran the few real opportunities he had to distinguish himself in this period. The shows were not so much pantomimes as topical revues built around a story or theme, consisting of songs, sketches and local jokes. Starting with a basic script, Jack and his fellow actors wrote much of their own material and were often given to improvisation.

The pantos rewarded him with a succession of roles that included a cigar-smoking infant, a marionette in a dollmaker's shop, an elf, a scarecrow and one of a quartet of Russian soldiers who had come to Ireland looking for the crown jewels. One year, in *Una agus Jimín*, he created a sensation by whistling his way through the entire performance.

It may be coincidence that his mime recalled Barrault's Baptiste; that the two can be compared is an indication of its quality.
— *The Sunday Press*, January 1950

There were times, however, when audiences had trouble taking MacGowran seriously. In *The Great Pacificator* he played a peasant lad, and was seen eating carrion in the last scene after killing a dog. One night a portion of the audience apparently found him comic rather than pathetic and laughed when they weren't supposed to.

"Jackie had a quality that made him at once funny and tragic. He couldn't do anything tragic without a sense of fun or absurdity in it," asserted actor Michael Clarke-Laurence, who worked with him at the Abbey and the Gate. "He had a kind of humor and grotesquerie about him which was an extraordinary gift." It was a gift that would serve MacGowran well, given the blend of tragic and comic elements in the plays of both Beckett and O'Casey.

When producer Ria Mooney permitted Jack to resuscitate the Abbey Experimental Theatre in the fall of 1948, he seized the opportunity. He collected a number of young actors who, like himself, were being given little to do, and began staging plays in the Peacock that were more challenging — and more nourishing — than the standard Abbey fare.

After handling a number of projects with satisfactory results, Mooney asked MacGowran to direct a play by the artist Jack B. Yeats. *In Sand* was a fantasy about an old man who leaves a legacy to a little girl, on her promise to write a remembrance of him in the sand of a beach. "It was a strange play. Nobody knew quite what to make of it, so it was given to Jackie to direct," recalled Grania O'Shannon, who played the lead.

Sensing the unusual nature of the material, MacGowran sought out Yeats. While Jack undoubtedly felt that personal contact with the man could bring about a richer understanding of the work, he was also curious about the author's older brother, William Butler Yeats.

Jack Yeats became a frequent visitor to rehearsals and sometimes went to tea with the company; such was his enthusiasm that he even

Courtesy of Micheál Ó Briain

The Abbey Players, 1947. *Standing, from left:* Ronnie Walsh, producer Michael J. Dolan, Joe Ellis, Michael Dunne, Doreen Madden, Father Leo McCann, Maureen Toal, Philip O'Flynn, Máire Ní Dhomhnaill, Brian O'Higgins, Bríd Ní Loinsigh, Harry Brogan. *Kneeling:* Sean Mooney, Geoff Golden, Jack MacGowran, Micheál Ó Briain.

designed sets for the production. MacGowran went to see Yeats regularly for further discussion at the artist's "winter quarters," the Portobello Nursing Home. The renowned painter was getting on in years, and the realization of one of his most ambitious creations pleased him immeasurably.

As MacGowran immersed himself in the production, the artistic vision in Yeats' canvases began to reveal itself in the play. He threw himself into the role of director feverishly, more intent on bringing Yeats' concepts to life than satisfying any creative whims of his own. MacGowran was particularly sensitive to the actor's point of view, and left himself open to any and all suggestions.

In Sand was met with hearty applause by the opening night audience on April 19, 1949. As the cast took their bow, Jack Yeats made his way to the stage. "I hope I have succeeded tonight in putting a little salt on the tail of the Peacock," he said. "To those of you who have not liked the play, I can only say, 'Ah! Well…!' To those of you who have liked it, may I say, 'Ah well, indeed!'"

The Irish Press called the opening "the most memorable in the Dublin theatre for a long time." The *Irish Times* observed, "It has established MacGowran as a producer of force and imagination." His supporters and detractors were unanimous in their praise of the eccentric young man — with the notable exception of Ernest Blythe, who called it "harmless rubbish."

"He disliked my very guts," MacGowran said in retrospect. "I made little or no headway, and I learned very little as an actor. We had great fun experimenting with plays of our own, but we were getting more attention than the Abbey, and the dear managing director promptly closed the Experimental Theatre down. He felt it was doing damage to the parent Abbey."

MacGowran's revival of the experimental program was hardly to blame for the ills that plagued the company. The damage done to the National Theatre by the loss of its preeminent actors and moreover its playwrights was irreparable; times had changed and the theatre, content to get by on its reputation, had failed to change with them. When poet Valentine Iremonger walked out on a performance of *The Plough and the Stars* decrying the management's "utter incompetence," *The Irish Times* could only endorse his protest.

The sterling acting talent that had characterized the earliest Abbey Players, the simplicity of movement and clarity of diction that fostered the legend of the Abbey acting tradition, had followed F.J. McCormick to the grave. Perfectionism had given way to what MacGowran later described as "competent mediocrity," and he found himself lacking.

Yearning to broaden his horizons, Jack set his sights on Paris and went to the French ambassador in Dublin. Once armed with a letter of introduction to Louis Jouvet, the doyen of French actors and producers, he joined the retainer staff of the Abbey — which guaranteed him a small salary — and went abroad.

"I learned about discipline in the Abbey all right, and realism in the theatre, but I felt we needed style," observed MacGowran. "We had a naturalism which came down through the Abbey's history, but a naturalism that had no style. I felt, a theatre that has such a background of style is Paris. I went over not to imitate their style, but to see if I could get something from them that I could add to our so-called naturalism."

The vibrant theatrical world of Paris confronted MacGowran with his comparative ignorance. In an effort to fill the gaps in his education he sought out the masters, studying not only with Jouvet at the Théâtre de l'Athenée, but producer André Barsacq and Jean-Louis Barrault, who allowed him to sit in on rehearsals of *Les Fourberies de Scapin* at the Atlier Marigny.

MacGowran worked at the Comédie-Française during his sojourn, and absorbed French theatre until he felt he had more or less developed "a style I could use." He also studied with Barrault's esteemed teacher, Étienne Decroux, who revived the lost art of pantomime and developed the language from which all modern technique derives.

While he had a natural sense of his body, MacGowran's decision to formally school himself in mime added immeasurably to his equipment — long before another former pupil, Marcel Marceau, caused actors from every corner of the globe to make the pilgrimage to Decroux's studio.

MacGowran's friends, however were not altogether impressed. "He was a great mime in the early days," recalled Dick O'Rafferty. "He had things he used to do at parties, like the one with the shopkeeper getting the bale of cloth for the woman. He wanted a few pals to see it after he'd been to Paris and taken lessons from Barrault. Some of the others, who had never seen it before, thought it was great. But to me it was spoiled, because now it was a performance. It was overdone."

But MacGowran was never to regret the lessons his fellow Abbey actors considered a luxury — not when he began to make a name for himself in London while they were still toiling anonymously at the Abbey; not when Samuel Beckett wrote a play for him to be performed wholly in mime; and not when Roman Polanski devised a starring role for him in a zany slapstick comedy. Nor did he regret the teachings of Barrault and Decroux years later when his performance in the BBC's award-winning *Silent Song* — as a Trappist monk under a vow of silence — caused *The Sunday Times* to remark:

> MacGowran's movement should be the envy of almost every actor in the world.

Such triumphs were far in the future when Jack returned from France. He made a strong impression on theatregoers and fellow actors alike as Rab, the Indian peddler, in Bryan MacMahon's *The Bugle in the Blood*. But the opportunities that followed this accomplishment were few. By the end of his third year at the Abbey Theatre, it was obvious to him that his future as an actor did not lie with the company. He went to the managing director and aired his grievances.

Blythe was short and to the point. "Accch, well you see, your nose is too big. And besides," he said, "there are not many parts for Indian peddlers."

3

The abiding impression MacGowran's former Abbey Theatre associates had of him was that of a dreamer. They recalled, in particular, the day he failed to show up for rehearsal and actor Brian O'Higgins quipped, "He's probably off in Paddy Dooley's, reading a book on the etiquette of the theatre."

Dim as his prospects may have been at the outset of his career, MacGowran looked at the bright side, in his own unique way. It was a quality that endeared him to many. "I remember Jack with deep affection," said actor Ronnie Walsh. "He could take a refreshing attitude toward any problem or situation. A flippant or irreverent remark from him could change a day that looked like it would be dreadful into one of hope and possibilities. He looked to the stars.

"With Jack around, there was always a plan to do a great production of something that would mean success for all. His one-man Beckett show was the realization of things we talked about earlier in our careers. I think Jack felt that what he achieved in later years justified his early searchings and deprivation."

The managing director of the Abbey never terminated MacGowran's contract, as the theatre had no formal contract with any of its players. But Ernest Blythe began to "create circumstances around him" — as one associate recalled — and Jack was moved to consider his alternatives. His appearance in the Abbey Christmas pantomimes for three years following is evidence that he left the theatre on relatively good terms, despite the management's lack of esteem for him.

Jack wrote to producer-playwright Edward Longford and asked if he might join Longford's prestigious company at the Dublin Gate Theatre. He was waiting for reply when Abbey producer Ria Mooney persuaded him to join the Radio Éireann Repertory Company instead.

MacGowran's fellow actors had taken to calling him "the new F.J. McCormick," claiming he had inherited the throne. But the accepted Abbey technique of watching and studying the veteran actors to see how they played the great parts was unacceptable to Jack. He didn't care to be the next McCormick, the next Charlie Chaplin or the next Jean-Louis Barrault, despite the frequent comparisons. He didn't want to live in their shadow; he wanted to be recognized for his own talents. He wanted to play the great parts, but he wanted to be an original.

Had he acted with Longford Productions, Jack might have received the training the Abbey failed to give him. Instead, he went into the Radio Éireann Rep where he found little satisfaction. There, unlike before, he was held back by his own inadequacies. He could communicate almost anything with his face and body but his speaking voice was thin and ineffective; he lacked vocal projection and depth.

Before long MacGowran was liberated from the Rep by British documentary filmmaker Paul Rotha, who came to Ireland in the summer of 1950 to make a drama about a family of gypsies. Rotha was intent on using actors suitable for the roles rather than stars; he plundered the Abbey, Gate and Radio Éireann companies in assembling his cast.

Jack was chosen to make his film debut in No *Resting Place* as Billy Kyle, one of the sons in the family. The director was relentless in his quest for realism, and MacGowran wanted to be as authentic in the part as a city boy could; he spent two months traveling with a band of gypsies or *tinkers*, living their itinerant life as part of his preparation for the role.

MacGowran returned to Dublin after three months filming on location in County Wicklow. He was 32 years old and decided it was time to leave home; if his mother was hospitable to the company he kept, his "bohemian friends" were less than welcome by his father. He and actor Godfrey Quigley moved into a flat in Fitzwilliam Street and christened it The Snake Pit. Jack's freedom from home was short-lived; his father visited the flat and told him he was a disgrace, insisting he move back home.

In the spring of 1951, MacGowran joined Hilton Edwards and Mícheál Mac Liammóir at the Gate Theatre. He had appeared in two productions with them when a group calling itself the Irish Players asked him to do O'Casey's *The Shadow of a Gunman* for a tour of American universities.

Two weeks into rehearsal for the tour, fate intervened. Academy Award- winning director John Ford arrived in Dublin with a crew of Hollywood technicians, his own stock company and a screenplay entitled *The Quiet Man*. He selected MacGowran for a featured role, augmented his cast with Abbey actors and headed west for Connemara. The American tour, with Milo O'Shea as Jack's replacement, was a disaster; the filmmaker, as usual, had a winner on his hands.

Ford, who started out in life as Sean O'Feeney, was born in Maine but had his roots deep in the rockstrewn soil of County Galway. The veteran director, whose efforts to film *The Plough and the Stars* had forever soured F.J. McCormick on Hollywood, knew full well he could not duplicate the rugged beauty of Ireland on a studio backlot.

Ford had made a handshake contract with John Wayne, Maureen O'Hara, Barry Fitzgerald and Victor McLaglen to do the picture in 1944, and had continued to work on the project for seven long years until he could get financing. He had a big stake in *The Quiet Man* and everything had to be exactly the way he wanted it; he demanded a certain discipline from his company and he got it.

The director had a strict rule that cast and crew would abstain from drinking while they were working on a picture. It was not an easy regulation to enforce; some of his favorite performers, including Wayne and McLaglen, were particularly heavy tipplers. MacGowran, who was cast as McLaglen's obnoxious little sidekick, would set a good example and be a positive influence in that regard — or so Ford hoped. "Jackie hardly takes a jar at all," an Abbey actor had assured him.

As it turned out, Wayne and McLaglen found a most willing accomplice and drinking partner in MacGowran. One night after a round of drinking, Jack was reprimanded by the director. He took off his coat and challenged Ford to a fight. A few smart-mouthed remarks followed when the challenge was denied. But Ford would not tolerate disrespect, and decided to make an example of MacGowran.

The next morning they were filming a scene where Wayne was to throw O'Hara's dowry money into a furnace. "You go stand up there!" yelled Ford, instructing MacGowran to stand with his back to the furnace. Jack had a dreadful hangover and the director knew it; he held himself upright by sheer willpower for three hours, swearing under his breath as the sweat poured from his brow. *You fucker, I'll show you. I'm not going to fall on my face.* When Ford thought he had suffered enough, he said, "I think you can move away now."

Leaving wet, green Ireland and its haphazard weather far behind, Ford returned to sunny California in mid-summer of 1951 to shoot his interior scenes on Hollywood soundstages. The townspeople of Cong, County Mayo — where many of the exteriors had been filmed — were astonished by the subsequent editing. "When John Wayne slugged Vic McLaglen in Hollywood, and he fell into the street in Cong — that was the first space shot," claimed a local shopkeeper.

When Ford had filmed his last scene at Republic Studios, MacGowran acquired an agent and sought additional work. But all of his hard-earned experience was of little consequence away from home. As he made the rounds of producers, they all had the same question: "What have you done?" One day the inevitable query came and the exasperated actor shot back, "Well, what have *you* done?"

The exception among producers was Gabriel Pascal, who promised Jack the starring role in his forthcoming film of Shaw's *Androcles*

In *The Quiet Man* with Maureen O'Hara, who grew up in the same Dublin neighborhood.

Courtesy of Gloria MacGowran

Siobhán McKenna, Jack MacGowran, Cyril Cusack, Dame Sybil Thorndyke and Maureen Cusack, during rehearsals for *The Playboy of the Western World*.

and the Lion. Little did MacGowran know that the producer had offered the part of Androcles to José Ferrer, Harpo Marx and every other actor he could think of, including Cantinflas. A promise meant absolutely nothing to Pascal.

Hollywood producers did not see MacGowran as a man who could play a wide variety of roles. They saw him as "a little green man" and that was what they wanted him to play — when they wanted him at all. Before long Jack departed, turning his back on their narrow attitudes and his own short-lived hope of becoming a "lens actor." Fate, with its curious sense of humor, brought him back seven years later — to play a leprechaun.

For all its appeal on the surface, MacGowran did not particularly enjoy his stay in the film capital. "We talked about Hollywood when he came back," said Dick O'Rafferty. "Everything was so permissive for him, a Synge Street boy. There was nothing of the charm of stolen fruit; everything was allowed. That spoiled it for him."

MacGowran grew restless once more on his return to Ireland. He went to London and tried to get a job with the Old Globe Theatre, the British Broadcasting Corporation — anything that would offer a change of pace. Michael Balcon eventually put him to work at Ealing Studios, casting him as an Irish nationalist in *The Gentle Gunman* and the scheming owner of a public transport company in *The Titfield Thunderbolt*.

Jack was more comfortable before a live audience than a motion picture camera, and he soon found himself back on stage, in the company of Hilton Edwards and Michéal Mac Liammóir. His tenure with the Dublin Gate Theatre would prove an education of the highest order.

Edwards and Mac Liammóir — to whom a teenaged Orson Welles had apprenticed himself two decades earlier — experimented with a variety of theatrical styles and concepts, limited only by their imagination, which proved infinite as the years passed. Mac Liammóir's flamboyant performances and rich costume designs, coupled with Edwards' revolutionary lighting and direction, had earned them a reputation without parallel in Ireland. At the close of every season, they traveled to Europe to observe firsthand the traditions and innovations of the theatre world at large.

While the Abbey forced severe restrictions on an actor with its "bacon and cabbage" repertoire of predominantly Irish plays, the Gate offered both actors and audiences a menu of what Mac Liammóir once called "dishes slightly more elaborately prepared" — the gamut of theatrical experiences, from Molnar and Strindberg to Cocteau and O'Neill. The Abbey promised an actor year-round security, but the

Gate was *the* place to learn the art of the theatre, as far as actors were concerned.

"Working with these two men in their company on a season-to-season basis was one of the greatest experiences an actor could have. If you had any intelligence at all, you had to acquire an enormous amount of knowledge observing those two men in action, an enormous amount of technique. There wasn't another company quite like it," noted Carroll O'Connor, who spent the early fifties at the Gate Theatre alongside MacGowran.

Gate actors labored long hours at their craft, intoxicated by the spell of the theatre. Unlike their counterparts at the Abbey, who scorned such talk, they never tired of discussing their work. "Jack loved acting, loved theatre people," recalled O'Connor. "He loved talking about plays, ruminating about what could be done, what he could do next. In those days, our lives in the theatre were almost totally theatre."

Pub-crawling and party-crashing were, however, the substance of an actor's life in Dublin, once the performance was over and the curtain had come down. MacGowran and his mates frequented Groom's Hotel across from the theatre in Parnell Square, Davy Byrne's in Duke Street — a favorite haunt of Beckett's, having been immortalized in Joyce's *Ulysses* — and Sinnott's in South King Street across from the Gaiety, where they sometimes put on shows. They would walk along Baggot Street late at night, assuming there was a party in progress wherever they saw a light burning. There were pubs that stayed open illegally and clubs that kept the lights on just for them. They never wanted the night — or the party — to end.

MacGowran's immoderate drinking was hardly unique in Dublin acting circles, but it was beginning to get in his way. The gentle, even-tempered pacifist — the life of the party when sober — became morose and sullen and sometimes belligerent under the influence; a latent hostility surfaced when he drank to excess. He was more often drunk than sober and his behavior was unpredictable. He could knock over a table of champagne or smash a friend's record collection and have no memory of it the next day.

He often went on stage with a hangover, but it rarely affected his performance. Jack and his fellow actors would get drunk in the morning, sleep it off in the afternoon and perform in the evening. A drink or two in the dressing room, between an exit and an entrance, was not unusual.

"Jack, in those days, was a man who loved to finish a show, get off the stage and have a few jars," remembered Michael Clarke-Laurence. "He loved that relaxation afterwards, those usual great Dublin conversations... the unfinished arguments, the jokes, the laughter, the novel to end all novels, the play that will make all play writing unnecessary for the entire future..."

MacGowran's opportunities at the Gate were limited in part by Hilton Edwards' disregard for his drinking. He won rave reviews for his portrayals of a cocky schoolmaster in Mac Liammóir's translation of *Dr. Knock*, the village eccentric in L.A.G. Strong's *The Director* and Roderigo in *Othello*, but his talents were underused, as at the Abbey.

In spite of the chameleon-like ability he had displayed in *Abraham Lincoln*, during the flu epidemic at the Gate a decade earlier, Jack was tailed by much the same problem that hindered him at the National Theatre. He was seldom considered for a role that could be played by someone else in the company.

"Here was this eccentric, gnomish fellow, a very definite talent, great willingness and keenness. But it was hard to cast Jackie in any ordinary way because he was physically abnormal looking," observed Edwards. "But he was unique. If you wanted that kind of thing, there was nobody as good. What I think pulled him out of the rut eventually was this uniqueness, this strange gnomish quality, and the fact that he hitched himself to the Beckett wagon."

If MacGowran failed to endear himself to either Edwards or his partner, they both retained great admiration and respect for him. "I personally never met anyone so ostentatiously ordinary as Jackie," asserted Micheál Mac Liammóir. "I don't mean 'ordinary' in the American sense; I mean it in the European sense — to me, he was like any other small talented actor. But he had something that obviously made an enormous appeal to many, many people. I've never known such an ordinary little fellow with so many lovers — and I don't mean in the French sense, necessarily."

MacGowran found new admirers in the Irish provinces when Cyril Cusack decided to present a revival of J.M. Synge's *The Playboy of the Western World* in the summer of 1953. Cusack cast Siobhán McKenna as the feisty Pegeen Mike, opposite himself as the cowardly hero, Christy Mahon. He asked MacGowran to play Siobhán's less worldly fiance, Shawn Keogh, and direct the show as well.

"I didn't want to direct it myself, and I knew that Jack would give a good account of himself," said Cusack. "He had a delicate touch; he gave the kind of direction that sensitive actors would respond to."

It was a landmark production, giving rural audiences their first opportunity to see the play that had so violently offended Dubliners at its Abbey première in 1907. "*The Playboy* had never been done in the provincial areas of Ireland so we were pioneering in a sense, doing the work the National Theatre was not doing," Cusack contended. "The play had been done in a rather over-subdued and introverted way previously; it hadn't breathed its fullest in our generation. Many people treated it as a sort of museum piece."

MacGowran took an innovative approach to Synge, giving free rein to his imagination. When he introduced music to the play, putting musicians on stage with melodian, flute and fiddle, there was dissent. Cusack objected to a lot of artistic choices MacGowran made, but Jack prevailed and won him over. Carroll O'Connor and other members of the cast felt he was making the right decisions, and Cusack deferred.

The group was appearing in Waterford when word came from London that Laurence Olivier wanted MacGowran and O'Connor to join his company. They thought it over and decided to remain with the tour. Then producer-director Mario Zampi made Jack and Carroll a tempting offer; he asked them to appear in a film with David Niven at a salary of £90 a week. Siobhán McKenna told them it would be a terrible thing to leave the tour; the actors did some soul searching and decided to remain with the company, although Cusack was paying them only £15 a week.

When the company finished their tour that summer, they were scheduled to continue on to the Festival of Nations in Paris. Instead, *The Playboy* ended its run in Galway with a wild party, and a vague yarn about why they were not going. Cusack later took the show to the First International Theatre Festival in France, where it was a huge success — except that MacGowran wasn't there. Save for his absence, the Paris production was identical to the one that had toured Ireland, yet Jack received no credit of any kind.

The injustice of the situation disturbed MacGowran greatly. "He was angry about not getting credit, and he was right too," conceded Cusack. "Jack had a fair grievance there. A great deal of the credit for our success was due to Jackie, for his direction of the play; he brought to it a great degree of artistry."

If MacGowran was distressed that someone else should receive credit for his work, it caused him more pain that he was never asked to play the bold-tongued Christy Mahon. Of the roles he was given early in his career, virtually all of them had one thing in common; his characters were odd or peculiar or in some way extraordinary.

When Hilton Edwards cast Jack as the Dauphin — the young prince destined to become King Charles VII — in the Gate's 1953 production of *Saint Joan*, he took a chance and cast against type. Shaw's Dauphin was, in the words of the playwright, "a poor creature physically... he has narrow little eyes, near together, a long pendulous nose

that droops over his thick short upper lip, and the expression of a
young dog accustomed to be kicked, yet incorrigible and irrepressible."

It was a difficult part, and some members of the cast wondered
during rehearsal whether MacGowran could pull it off. But Siobhán
McKenna, who starred opposite him as Joan, had no doubt whatever.
"Jackie looked *exactly* as Shaw describes the character," she said.

Saint Joan was taken down to Limerick and Cork and up to Belfast
early in 1954, a tour made memorable by offstage events. McKenna's
suite in Limerick's Desmond Hotel had a bigger living room than some
of the others, and one night wardrobe man Paul Smith asked if he could
use it to serve drinks to MacGowran and actor Denis Brennan.
McKenna agreed, but told them to keep the noise down.

Their boisterous conversation kept her awake, however, so she
asked them to leave. Brennan left the room; MacGowran asked if he
could sleep on the floor with Siobhán's dog, Topsy. Smith, who was on
his way out, decided to create a little drama, and told Denis that Jack
was trying to climb into bed with Siobhán.

Brennan rushed into the room and punched MacGowran in the
mouth, knocking out one of his front teeth. The actors splattered blood
everywhere as they crawled around, looking for the tooth — Jack had
read that it would grow back, if it was put in place immediately.

The following night MacGowran performed with a badly swollen
lip, and a wad of gum in place of the missing tooth. His speech was
almost incomprehensible. When Hilton Edwards demanded to know
what happened, Jack replied, "I walked into a lamp post."

Some years later, Edwards called McKenna and asked her to
reprise *Saint Joan* for the Paris theatre festival and a European tour. She
told him there was only one Dauphin. "It must be Jackie," she insisted.
Micheál Mac Liammóir took the phone and informed her that he was
going to play the part. McKenna protested: "You were never a Bisto
kid."

Mac Liammóir won the role — out of sheer stubborness — but lost
the argument. He was the first to admit he bore no resemblance to the
hungry waif pictured on advertisements for Bisto Soup. "Siobhán said
I was too beautiful to play the Dauphin," he remembered. "What she
meant was, I was too old. She felt she couldn't mother me, like she
could Jackie."

McKenna eventually took the play all over the world, but never
found anyone else who could play the role to her satisfaction. "I
compared every other actor who played the part with Jackie," she said.
"He would never play a line for a cheap laugh, like the others did. In
the cathedral scene, for instance, he says of Joan, 'I wish she'd keep

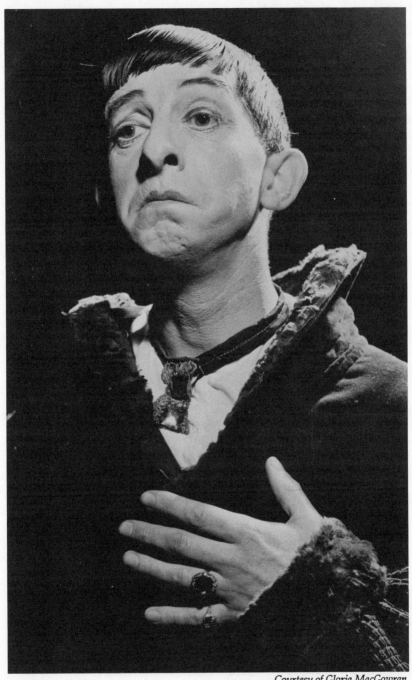

The man who would be king: As the Dauphin in the 1953 Dublin Gate
Theatre production of Shaw's *Saint Joan*.

Hilton Edwards, Siobhán McKenna and Micheál Mac Liammóir, in a celebratory mood.

Backstage with Treasa Nic Oirella, Denis Brennan and Michael O'Herlihy. Gaiety Theatre, Dublin, 1953.

quiet and go home' — every other actor went for the laugh. Jackie said it in a thoughtful, reflective way; he showed the side that made Charles a great king afterwards.

"Jackie was full of surprise," said McKenna. "You never knew how he was going to play a role. He liked to get into the character's skin rather than twist a character to his own personality."

Denis Brennan, who played Dunois, recalled Mac Liammóir's portrayal as "an actor's performance, very theatrical. It didn't come close to Jack's — he was totally believable, this childish, unthinking prince who would not have been crowned but for Joan."

MacGowran was on tour with the show when the Cork Opera House invited him to do a production for their annual festival, *An Tóstal*. He decided to form his own company, together with Brennan, Godfrey Quigley and Gate designer Michael O'Herlihy. The four of them felt there was room for another theatre in town; they wanted more freedom than Edwards allowed them and they were tired of fending off Mac Liammóir's sexual advances.

In a press release filled with lofty idealism, the fledgling entrepreneurs announced their intention "to turn Ireland's dramatic significance outwards, to integrate Ireland in world drama." They made their debut with Padraic Fallon's *The Seventh Step* in April 1954, borrowing money from private investors to stage the play.

The quartet called themselves the Dublin Globe Theatre. Hilton Edwards had another name for them — "Alcoholics Unanimous." They were, in any case, a collection of individual artistic temperaments who quickly realized they could not work together in harmony. MacGowran and Quigley soon found themselves at odds with each other, a personality clash that escalated into a full-scale rivalry between the former roommates. They would get into rows over which of them was more Irish; when Brennan suggested that MacGowran play Cyrano in a Globe production, Quigley immediately vetoed the idea.

His differences with Quigley and O'Herlihy clearly irreconcilable, MacGowran felt he had reached a dead end in Dublin. He had worked with the Abbey and the Gate, and apart from an odd moment of glory, found little satisfaction in either experience. He had formed his own company, only to see the association dissolve over personal disparities. There was nothing more he could do but go into exile.

Paddy Dooley, the tobacconist, loaned Jack a few pounds and smuggled him on the ferry at Dun Loaghire, and he was on his way to London. At long last, the restless young actor had finally succeeded in severing himself artistically from the repressive climate of "that fuckin' mother-ridden country" — as he called it — that had driven so many native sons from its soil.

4

If the snakes driven out of Ireland by Saint Patrick swam to New York and joined the police force — as Eugene O'Neill once sagely observed — actors driven out by lack of gainful employment in the fifties often swam to London and found work in revivals of Irish plays. They were so well suited to the parts that British producers gave them little chance to do anything else, and often there was no employment at all. Still, they preferred starving in London to stagnating in Dublin.

MacGowran made his London stage debut on May 27, 1954, as the Young Covey in *The Plough and the Stars*. The intense, angry Covey in Sean O'Casey's dramatization of the 1916 Easter Rebellion was the personification of young O'Casey himself — a part Jack had long coveted. He invested it with a fervor and passion that made a solid impression on critics and theatregoers alike, but failed to generate great demand for his talents afterwards.

Jack lived in London's Chelsea district during the mid-fifties, in a flat that was an almost ideal set-up. His Irish landlady was always willing to fix the struggling actor a meal, and never worried how late the rent was. But MacGowran wanted desperately to make a success of himself in those days, and he exerted no undue amount of pressure on himself. Things were so bad he was often tempted to return to Dublin, but he couldn't go back having failed to succeed in London.

He did go back to Ireland for the occasional movie role, notably *The Rising of the Moon*, in which John Ford cast him as a maker of illicit *poteen* whiskey. MacGowran had not forgotten the run-in with the "very ruthless but very human" director during *The Quiet Man*, but he could voluntarily abstain from neither the boozing nor the all-night card games on location in Connemara.

Jack forgot he had an early schedule one day and waltzed in late, the tell-tale evidence in his eyes. The director borrowed a teetotaler's pin from a crew member and stuck it into MacGowran. "From now on," said Ford, "you're the pioneer on this picture — no more drinking."

Back in London, Jack found work as a commentator for the Irish edition of Universal News and won the occasional part on BBC Radio. He played the lead in a broadcast of Jack Yeats' *In Sand* but was unable to revive the stage production that had won him such acclaim in

Dublin. Try as he might, his opportunities were few. The British thought of him strictly as an *Irish* actor, while MacGowran considered himself an actor who happened to be Irish.

In desperation, Jack decided to capitalize on his nationality. He formed his own Irish Players in the fall of 1956 and staged O'Casey's *The Shadow of a Gunman* at the New Lindsey, showcasing himself as the shameless Seamus Shields. The lazy, unwashed, self-respecting coward of a war-torn Dublin — a part created by F.J. McCormick at the Abbey — was a natural for MacGowran, and he wore it with confidence. Glowing notices from prestigious London critics like Kenneth Tynan and Harold Hobson confirmed his gifts.

The Kensington Post summed up his triumph:

> MacGowran is in his element with the wild, poetic, philosophical O'Casey prose — and the audiences love him.

The Irish Players could not raise enough capital to follow Tynan's suggestion that they transfer the play to the vibrant theatre district in the West End. Jack's agent however came up with enough cash to put the show on in the Lyric, Hammersmith. MacGowran shared the spotlight there with a spectacular set created by Sean Kenny, a new-found friend who would soon become a sought-after stage designer.

Jack also struck up a friendship with Sean O'Casey during this period, and often visited the playwright at his home in Torquay, Devon. He went initially to talk about O'Casey's work, but they found much in common; they discussed world literature and drama at length, and often delighted in singing ballads into the early hours of the morning. They talked long into the twilight of the Ireland they had left — as had so many before them — seeking a fulfillment they could not find in the repressive environment there.

MacGowran came away broadened and exhilarated by his visits with O'Casey. "From his writings many people thought him narrow and bitter, but he was the antithesis of these things. He wrote with rage about narrow institutions because he himself was broad in mind... he was a wonderfully expansive man to talk to, full of good humor," said MacGowran. "He wanted to create joy and be surrounded by joy. He used his plays as a platform for this belief and never gave up until the end of his days."

The actor thought he had "arrived" on the London stage with *The Shadow of a Gunman*, but he soon found otherwise. The play closed after a few weeks at the Lyric, and he went back on National Assistance — unaware that he was about to embark on a long and fruitful association with another countryman, a disciple of James Joyce who now resided in Paris.

As Seumas Shields, with Desmond Jordan in *The Shadow of a Gunman*.
London, 1956.

MacGowran was aware that there was something more than a little
peculiar about Samuel Beckett, or at least about his work. For one, he
couldn't get the words out of his head. The day before *Shadow* reo-
pened at the Lyric, he had performed in a radio play by Beckett called
All That Fall. His role — that of Tommy, a porter in a rural Irish railway
station — was not a large one, but he found himself utterly fascinated.
Haunted by the strange, interior rhythms and sparing use of
language, he soon began to immerse himself in the author's work. "I
was struck tremendously by the writing," recalled MacGowran. "It
seemed to me to be profound, and yet ironically funny, in a style I'd
never come across before. I didn't know then who Beckett was — I'd
never heard of him. I thought he was a Frenchman whose work had
been translated into English."

Only later would he learn that Samuel Beckett had taught French at Trinity College in Dublin, before leaving Ireland to wander throughout Europe. The 50-year-old author's small but growing reputation was then based on a trilogy of post-war novels originally written in French, and only just being published in English — and a play called *Waiting for Godot*, which had been recently performed in London to the sometimes hostile reception of baffled public.

Beckett had been taken by surprise when the British Broadcasting Corporation asked him to consider writing an original play for radio. The idea appealed to him, but he knew instinctively that he could not write to order; nor did he wish to be pinned down to a deadline.

While he was at work on *All That Fall*, Beckett chanced to hear a BBC radio broadcast of Michael Molloy's *The Paddy Pedlar*, starring MacGowran and J.G. Devlin. He was intrigued by their voices, and asked producer Donald McWhinnie to cast them in the play.

The author's first venture into radio drama was met with the sort of critical reaction he had come to expect:

> It takes hold on the imagination as compellingly as did its theatrical forerunner [*Waiting for Godot*], it is as hard to interpret satisfactorily and it plumbs the same pessimistic depths in what seems a no less despairing search for human dignity.
>
> — *The Times*, January 14, 1957

Beckett refused to travel to England for the production, preferring to let the work speak for itself. He came to London in March, however, to sit in on rehearsals for the world première of his second stage play, *Fin de partie (Endgame)*.

MacGowran meanwhile was becoming so involved in his work that "I had to meet the man. It wasn't just idle curiosity — it was a compulsion," he told an interviewer. "At that time Beckett's work was difficult to understand and I thought finding out his way of life and thinking might add a dimension to the writing." At MacGowran's request, Donald McWhinnie introduced them in the bar of the dreary Royal Court Hotel where Beckett was staying, and left them alone.

Jack was terrified. He didn't know what to say, except that he wanted to "meet the man." He was unaware that the tall, lanky author was equally shy, and felt even more awkward at meeting him.

Beckett ordered a bottle of whiskey. When the management refused to serve him a bottle, he asked for perhaps two dozen glasses. In wordless confrontation they sat drinking Irish whiskey and lager, the humble, reticent poet; the frightened, reverent actor. MacGowran admired the man so much, he couldn't think of a thing to say.

Beckett stared at the floor. The silence grew intense. MacGowran grew embarrassed and suddenly blurted out something about a rugby match.

"Ah, wasn't that a great match!" exclaimed Beckett. For two hours they chatted enthusiastically about rugby, golf, cricket and six-day bike riding; the subject of literature — much less the writer's work — never came up. MacGowran thought he was "talking rubbish," but Beckett found the conversation so stimulating he never made it to the theatre that night.

When they were both sufficiently drunk, the actor looked his companion in the eye. "I detect tones of Dublin," he said.

"You're right," said Beckett. Only then did MacGowran discover that the author was not — as he had thought all along — "a French provincial who had picked up a Gaelic lilt."

MacGowran himself then had a lilt to his speech that was interfering with the progression of his career — at least as far as he was concerned. Determined to break away from the stereotype that held him back, he set out to lose the rich Dublin accent that had so charmed the London critics. He also took voice lessons and worked to improve his diction, so that he sounded a little less Irish and a little more cosmopolitan.

As Jack began to develop his voice, the demand for his talents began to increase. While the BBC called him regularly for radio work — mostly O'Casey plays — television gave him the opportunity to first fully display his abilities to a vast audience. He distinguished himself on TV during this period as Emile, the strange, decrepit butler in Anouilh's *Dinner With the Family*, and Huish, the Cockney pirate, in *Ebb Tide*. Still he suffered long bouts of unemployment.

MacGowran could become hugely depressed when he was not working. The sanctity of the theatre and the shelter of the pub were, in effect, the only refuge from his private demons. To while away the weeks and often months that passed between acting assignments, the actor frequented such establishments as The Queen's Elm in Chelsea and Gerry's Club in the theatre district. He was also a regular at The George — better known to its clientele as "The Glue Pot" — where he rubbed elbows with BBC associates and matched pint for pint with Brendan Behan and poet Louis MacNeice.

Behan, who didn't get along with Irish bartenders and was often thrown out of The George, shared with MacGowran the quality of being unembarrassed when drunk. It was a quality which stood both of them in good stead. On one occasion when he was sober, the playwright put MacGowran to bed with a lecture on the evils of alcohol —

In a movie role, about the time he began his association with Samuel Beckett in 1957.

but rarely were either of them sober in each other's company.

If Jack generally had "the price of admission" into a public house, he could not always pay his rent. He and actor Donal Donnelly were sharing a flat in Lancaster Road — "a tatty little place, but only £2, 10 shillings a week," recalled Donnelly — when MacGowran received the phone call that would change his luck in London.

Director Peter Wood wanted the actor for the part of the burned-out anarchist, Larry Slade, in his production of *The Iceman Cometh*. MacGowran was living on National Assistance and working in a ketchup factory; he rejected the offer. Instead, he suggested he take the role of Harry Hope, the irascible pub owner. Wood apologized — the part had already been cast — and terminated the conversation.

Jack could ill afford to turn down any acting job at this point, much less a central role in a Eugene O'Neill play. But he saw no point in going off welfare to play Slade. He didn't feel he could make a success of the part, and preferred to scramble along rather than take something that wasn't right.

A few days later Wood called and said he'd like to further discuss the matter. On a whim, MacGowran suggested they meet in the middle of Westminister Bridge; there, suspended above the cold, quiet waters of the Thames they talked it over. Jack had waited months for a good part to come along, and his gamble paid off.

Harry Hope, the cranky old codger in whose rundown saloon the play takes place, hasn't set foot outside the premises in 20 years. O'Neill characterized him as "so thin the description 'bag of bones' was made for him... he has the face of an old family horse, prone to tantrums." MacGowran went back to his youth in fleshing out the part. Chief among his stage mannerisms was a peculiar way of looking through his glasses that recalled his nearsighted Aunt Daisy.

"In a kind of funny way, as we went through rehearsal, Jackie became more and more like Harry Hope — you could actually see it. When he finally did it, it was absolutely extraordinary. I don't expect to see anyone do it as well again, ever," said Patrick Magee, who disliked his own performance as Slade.

"He got his marvelous, curious feeling by putting on the glasses, which he couldn't see through. But the best thing he did was when he went outside the saloon to have a pee. Jackie was very good at that sort of thing, the mime. And the extraordinary thing, out of this tiny body the enormous voice."

The curtain went up on O'Neill's burned-out dreamers on January 29, 1958, at London's intimate Arts Theatre Club. The play, which ran over four hours, was a rousing success; it soon transferred to the West

As Phadrig Oge, right, in *Darby O'Gill and the Little People.*

End, where it had a long and healthy engagement at the Winter Garden.

Kenneth Tynan, who kept his finger firmly on the pulse of British theatre in the fifties and sixties, criticized O'Neill's "ginmill dialogue," but pinpointed his greatness when he summed up the play's appeal: "He is one of the few writers who can enter, without condescension or contempt, the world of those whom the world has rejected.

"Jack MacGowran, pinch-faced and baggy-trousered, plays the proprietor with a weasel brilliance I have not seen since the heyday of F.J. McCormick," observed Tynan, who hailed him as one of the best young actors on the London stage. MacGowran was voted the Best Supporting Actor of the Year award in the 1957-58 Variety Poll of drama critics — an accolade sweetened by the fact that he turned down the role originally offered him.

When *The Iceman Cometh* ended its run, Jack made his second trip to Hollywood. Walt Disney had cast MacGowran's boyhood idol, comedian Jimmy O'Dea, as the 5,000-year-old king of the leprechauns in *Darby O'Gill and the Little People*; Jack was signed to play his lieutenant, Phadrig Oge. The salary was more attractive than the role.

While he spent a lot of time socializing with friends from the days of *The Quiet Man*, the Disney assignment did not make for a pleasant visit. Having to follow his stage success with an insignificant movie role was depressing enough; the part itself was even more demoralizing. MacGowran was incensed at being cast as "a little green man" — having finally escaped the stereotype in London. As a result, he drank to excess; he was nearly fired off the film after having a run-in with Disney himself during a costume fitting.

Jimmy O'Dea invested the film with great fun, but he did not enjoy the job any more than MacGowran. He was getting on in years and the extra harsh light required to photograph them as miniatures made the film a grueling chore. The happiest part of the experience for both of them was the long voyage home — when they discovered that the ship's cabins had been liberally stocked with vodka, courtesy of Disney Productions.

His career having catapulted from the sublime to the ridiculous, MacGowran now moved back to the sublime — or sublimely ridiculous: the first British English-language production of Samuel Beckett's *Endgame*.

Perhaps the harshest of Beckett's plays, "even worse" and "more inhuman" than *Waiting for Godot* — according to the playwright — *Endgame* focuses on a love-hate relationship between two men in a room. The blind, paralyzed Hamm and the maimed, misshapen Clov, who attends to his every whim, are players in what Beckett once described as a "chess game lost from the start." From the outset Beckett dismissed any and all interpretations of the play by others, having "no elucidations to offer of mysteries that are all of their own making."

Harold Hobson defended the author's reticence from the beginning:

> Mr. Beckett is a poet; and the business of a poet is not to clarify, but to suggest, to imply, to employ words with auras of association, with a reaching out towards a vision, a probing down into an emotion, beyond the compass of explicit definition.
> — *The Sunday Times*, April 7, 1957

The English-language version of *Endgame* — which was to have been presented in London prior to *Fin de partie* — was delayed a year and a half, initially by Beckett's inability to translate it to his satisfaction, and subsequently by censorship problems. While Beckett felt that the English translation was, inevitably, "a poor substitute for the original," and lacked the sharpness it had in French, he permitted *Endgame* to be staged at the Royal Court Theatre in the fall of 1958.

Beckett was dissatisfied with the original French production at the Court by Roger Blin; the actors were imposing their own ideas and their timing was off. George Devine, who directed the English version and played Hamm — opposite MacGowran as Clov — was more polite than Blin but no more capable of giving Beckett what he wanted.

Avoiding the tension that had characterized the rehearsal period with Blin, Beckett supervised Devine's production with reserve and hesitation. "Sam didn't involve himself then as he did later," said Donald McWhinnie, whose première production of Beckett's *Krapp's Last Tape* shared the bill at the Court.

"Beckett had a suggestion and he wanted me to pass it on. I told him to tell George. Sam said, 'No, I can't criticize.' I told him if he didn't, no one else was going to," noted McWhinnie. "I said, 'If it isn't right, you must tell him.' Sam was like a child; he felt it wasn't his place to impose."

Devine, who revered Beckett, cast himself as the despotic Hamm only after Alec Guinness refused the part. The distinguished actor-producer became unnerved by the responsibilities he had heaped upon his shoulders, and ultimately felt he had failed the playwright.

MacGowran found little rapport with Devine, whom he felt was all wrong for the role — "too avuncular." For his own part, Jack did not entirely understand the sad, slavish Clov. He was not at all sure of himself as he made his way through the convolutions of this bleakest of black comedies, and was wholly unsatisfied with his performance.

The actor was often his own worst critic. "Jackie was impeccable in the way he worked. He didn't have great confidence in himself, though. He didn't know the effect he was creating — that's why he was good," asserted director Tony Richardson, who ran the Royal Court with Devine.

"Beckett's characters live in the mind rather than the real world. It requires an extraordinary gift to embody someone like Clov — it requires a particular kind of poetry of acting, or poetry of personality. It's difficult to define; it's not something you can relate to naturalistic terms," said Richardson. "An actor needs to respond, to see the Beckett vision. To have that strange, poetic kind of thing that makes it work is very rare. Jackie had it."

Devine did not. He was accused of humanizing the play by some, while applauded for it by others. Some critics found his production more palatable than *Fin de partie*; others felt it was more tedious than ever, dismissing the play as "weird and wanton drivel." In praise or blame, the press found it greatly at variance with Blin's version:

> The French production... was bitter and utterly pessimistic while [Devine's] had undergone a softening-down process and was, in consequence, not so depressing. It was also slower and funnier. But this humanising was to our mind a mistake. The play tended to become a bit of a bore and one couldn't help wishing, like Hamm, that "it would all end soon."
> — *Theatre World*, December 1958

Theatregoers themselves were neither willing nor able to see the vision that was Beckett's in the fifties. Audiences at the Royal Court often felt the avant garde plays put on there were unfit for the stage; they were frequently shocked or offended by what they saw and did not hesitate to walk out. *Endgame* was no exception.

Hamm: Clov!
Clov: Yes.
Hamm: Have you not had enough?
Clov: Yes! (*Pause*.) Of what?
Hamm: Of this... this... thing.
Clov: I always had. (*Pause*.) Not you?
Hamm: (*gloomily*) Then there's no reason for it to change.
Clov: It may end. (*Pause*.) All life long the same questions, the same answers.

By the midpoint of the lengthy one-act play, the majority of the audience had had more than enough of "this thing" Beckett had wrought and couldn't wait to find out how — or *if* — it would end. Devine and MacGowran found themselves playing to the sound of empty seats slapping back, as theatregoers marched out in droves. The sound of people snoring was also familiar to them.

One night a man stood up in the stalls and made himself conspicuous. "I've had enough of this garbage!" he declared. MacGowran timed his response as carefully as a line of dialogue. "Sir —" he roared, as the man reached the back of the house, "it may be garbage to you — but it took me one goddamn long time to learn it!"

If Jack found the audience's reception wanting, and his own performance lacking, the 1958 *Endgame* was significant in that it helped to cement a bond between MacGowran and Beckett. "They got very close at that time," confirmed Donald McWhinnie, who fondly recalled a "booze-up" hosted by actor Richard Goolden, who played Hamm's decrepit father, Nagg.

"We all got pretty smashed, and Jackie was paralytic. We came out of Goolden's flat and he passed out," said the director. "I have this vivid image of Sam picking Jackie up in his arms and carrying him like a baby through the streets."

5

During the run of *Endgame* at the Royal Court, an acquaintance of MacGowran's — a young actor on the way up named Peter O'Toole — was a frequent backstage visitor. One night he brought an attractive blonde with him, an avid reader of Beckett whose concept of the play varied sharply from what she had seen on stage.

O'Toole introduced her to MacGowran, who asked her to wash his hair. She would later recall having seen the same actor as Harry Hope, and years earlier as the Dauphin in *Saint Joan*, though she had no idea who he was. Nor did she divulge her identity to him; that she was a native of County Westmeath, Ireland, and the younger daughter of Irish baronet Sir Walter Nugent — who had campaigned for Home Rule for Ireland with Parnell — was not something Aileen Gloria Nugent went around telling everyone. "I didn't want people to know who I was," she said later. "I wanted to be liked for myself."

Gloria MacGowran recalled vividly the night she met her future husband, late in 1958. "He had all this silver stuff in his hair from playing Clov, so I washed his hair and then everybody went back as per usual to my flat," she said. "There were about 40 people there that night. Suddenly we heard screams. My sister-in-law had just come out of the bath and Jack decided he wanted to have her. Mainly he didn't like her; when he was drinking he had absolutely X- ray eyes.

"Suddenly he turned from being really fun to really nasty. He came over and hit me. I was used to it; I had grown up with it. I just said, 'Why did you do that?' And he just looked at me. Then Jack went over to the piano and swept everything off with his hand, and I thought, 'This is going a bit too far.' I went over and said, 'You'll have to go.' He was swaying back and forth, and he looked at me for a long time. He said, 'All right, princess,' and he left."

MacGowran was drunk when they met for the second time, backstage a few nights later. "At that time he was living with some dame, and he played that night with a broken tooth," recalled Gloria. "He was drinking a cup of tea, and she bashed it into his face and broke his tooth and cut his lip. After the show he was shaking and crying; he was in a very bad state."

Jack invited himself to spend the night at Gloria's flat, and the next day he told her he wanted to live with her. She protested that he didn't even know her. "I know you," he insisted, "and I'd like to live with you." But Gloria was adamant. "That's not possible," she said, "because you're already living with somebody else and you don't know me and I don't know you."

The 40-year-old actor was supposed to leave for New York in less than a week, to do a Broadway show. He wanted to move his belongings from the residence he shared with the other woman, and Gloria agreed to look after them while he was away. The night he was scheduled to leave, they surreptitiously collected his things, dropped them off and went to the airport. But Jack boarded the plane only after his jilted girlfriend managed to detain him for several hours, by claiming he'd stolen her passport.

MacGowran made his first trip to New York that winter at the behest of Sean O'Casey, to appear in a musical based on *Juno and the Paycock*. A more youthful O'Casey might well have rejected the idea of having his intrinsically Irish drama reworked into such an American aberration, but he was getting on in years and wanted to leave some money for his wife.

O'Casey, who had never taken money to write what his heart was not in, had only to sell the rights; the adaptation was left to others. Shirley Booth, the star of *Come Back Little Sheba*, was signed to play the indomitable Juno; veteran stage and film actor Melvyn Douglas hesitantly agreed to co-star as her lazy, irresponsible husband, Captain Boyle.

Casting Boyle's parasitic drinking companion, the spineless Joxer Daly, proved a difficult task for the producers. They contacted Siobhán McKenna and asked for suggestions. "Jackie MacGowran's your man," she told them. MacGowran had played the part in his amateur days, and more recently on BBC Radio.

Sean O'Casey was not only agreeable to the proposal, he insisted on it. The more he thought about the idea, the more he liked it. He went so far as to have it written into his contract that Jack *had* to play Joxer, and there could be no substitution; no MacGowran, no musical.

Daarlin' Man went into rehearsal at the Henry Miller Theater in December 1958, with an army of singers and dancers, a full-scale orchestra and some 20 production numbers. Overburdened with superfluous scenes — as well as jigs, ballets and barbershop harmonies — the simple artistry of O'Casey was lost.

Joseph Stein's book was one problem; Marc Blitzstein's music and lyrics were another. In adapting the play — which is set in a Dublin tenement during the Irish civil war — they became preoccupied with a number of cute songs that had nothing to do with the story. What they were doing to O'Casey's masterpiece was enough to infuriate anyone with any feeling for the original; it was enough to drive them to drink — literally. When MacGowran drank, he said exactly what he felt, with a boldness he otherwise lacked.

One morning during rehearsal, a row broke out between creative powers. Joe Stein told director Vincent J. Donehue he had to eliminate a piece of business, because it ruined a scene. Choreographer Agnes de Mille insisted things had to remain as they were; her dancers were coming on next. Marc Blitzstein argued that the score had to have a breather. The rehearsal came to a standstill as the ruckus escalated. Finally, MacGowran blew a fuse.

"Just a *fuckin'* minute," he yelled, in a broad Dublin tongue. There was dead silence in the house. He turned and looked at his associates from the stage.

"There's not a fuckin' one o' you down there that knows a fuckin' thing about Sean O'Casey, or this fuckin' play. You've no fuckin' conception o' what the play said, o' what the man is sayin', o' what the actors should be sayin'. Now would you please decide which fuckin' one o' you is gonna direct this fuckin' mess, and then let *me* know — and I'll do whatever the fuck he says!"

The irrepressible actor was called on the carpet for his outburst, but apologetic he was not; he could not and would not tolerate what was being done to something he loved and had grown up with. Producer Roger L. Stevens might have let him go then and there but the actor was protected by the clause in O'Casey's contract, and he knew it. Jack looked around the room, and then at director Donehue. "Sack him," he suggested.

MacGowran was staying in a one-room apartment as the guest of an old Dublin pal, Michael McAloney, and his wife Donna. McAloney tried to keep him sober during the day, but was unable to restrain him after rehearsal. One night, after they were thrown out of P.J. Clarke's saloon for singing, Jack's hosts took him home and put him to bed.

"He had a very bad night," recalled McAloney. "He sat up in bed and he said to me, 'Mick, there's little tiny lions all over the end of my bed. Will you get them out of here?' I put my arms around Jackie and told him there were no lions. We got that calmed down but he was still thrashing around, and he fell out of bed and hit a trunk and cracked a couple of ribs. But he was so drunk he didn't feel it."

The next morning, MacGowran was rehearsing a duet with Melvyn Douglas. On cue, Douglas picked up his lightweight co-star by the shoulders and lifted him onto the dining room table.

"Oh, Jaaaysus!" screamed MacGowran, grabbing at his chest as he

Photo by Fred Fehl

Disaster on Broadway: Melvyn Douglas and Jack MacGowran, as Captain Boyle and Joxer Daly, in the ill-fated production of *Juno*. New York, 1959.

was hoisted into the air. He decided he was having a heart attack. The producers rushed him to the hospital, but found nothing wrong with his heart. That evening he felt sufficiently recovered to attend a party with his understudy, Tom Clancy; they ran into a doctor friend of Tommy's who examined Jack, found the damage and taped up his ribs.

"The scene where we had to climb up on the table got to be a very hazardous experience night after night," recalled Melvyn Douglas, who relied on MacGowran to help him with his Dublin accent. "Jack and I became great friends, even though I had to practically carry him through most of the performances.

"On a number of occasions, by the time we got to the finish where we were all prancing around on stage, Jack literally hung onto me. It may have been obvious to some of the other members of the company, but everyone was so enchanted with the man, and his performance, that no offense was taken at it."

The show — by now called *Juno* — was no more steady on its feet than MacGowran when it premièred in Washington, D.C., in mid-January. The critics overlooked some of its flaws but readily attacked others; they felt O'Casey's earthy characters, with the notable exception of MacGowran's Joxer, had been "turned from substance to shadow."

At the opening night party, Roger Stevens began lecturing Jack about his drinking. The producer went on at length; MacGowran listened patiently until the harangue was over. "Mr. Stevens," he said, "have you read the fuckin' reviews? 'Cause that's the fuckin' answer, isn't it? Drunk or sober I'm the only fuckin' one gettin' 'em."

MacGowran's drinking scared some of his associates; his talent put a fright into others. Drunk or sober the sharp-tongued Irishman was too much. The actor's contract said nothing about the *size* of his part, so the producers retaliated by cutting a number of his scenes. When Marc Blitzstein wrote a song for Jack, Shirley Booth insisted they cut it; when the notices came in they trimmed his role still further. There was precious little left, but Jack was unperturbed. "You can cut it to the barest bones," he boasted, "and I'll still make Joxer live."

The company left Washington at the end of the month and went on to Boston. When they opened at the Shubert Theater, the critics were merciless. By the third day Vinnie Donehue had left the production and José Ferrer was brought in as his replacement. He and Jack found an instant rapport.

On the train to New York some weeks later, MacGowran got into a lively discussion about *Juno and the Paycock* with Tom Clancy and Liam Lenihan, the two other Irish members of the cast. Shirley Booth overheard them and began asking questions — the producers had told her *not* to read O'Casey; it would only confuse her. She read the original play that night and called Ferrer to tell him she wanted out.

Booth was talked into remaining with the company, which trouped into the Winter Garden Theatre March 9, 1959, two weeks behind schedule. Once more they were roasted by the press.

> O'Casey makes his own music; the words themselves sing and require no outside help ...I can perhaps sum up my feeling about *Juno* by saying that my heart sank whenever the conductor raised his baton.
> — *The New Yorker*, March 21, 1959

Juno closed after 16 performances on Broadway, much to the surprise of many who had seen it — but not to the cast. "I didn't really feel at home in the thing from the outset," conceded Melvyn Douglas. "I was right from the start a little doubtful about the wisdom of trying to do it as a musical; it seemed to me such a perfect piece of work in its own right that there wasn't much point in fiddling with it.

"We got nowhere with Vincent Donehue at all. But I think the trouble was much more basic than anything that could be done with it," said Douglas. "I don't think it would've made all that much difference if José Ferrer had directed the show from the beginning."

If MacGowran's U.S. stage debut was a debacle, the critics loved him. "They could never have found him in a casting office," marveled Elliot Norton of *The Boston Record American*. "He is the living lying image of Joxer Daly, merry and malicious." *Newsweek's* critique was the topper:

> Melvyn Douglas as the sly, strutting "paycock" and Shirley Booth as the braggart's acerb, patient wife are talented players, but only Jack MacGowran, as the toadying Joxer Daly, could conceivably be at home in the pubs and tenements of O'Casey's Dublin.

MacGowran tried to parlay his notices into another job when the show closed, but was unable to capitalize on them. He tried and failed to get a part in *Finian's Rainbow* before heading back to London, where he took up residence in a hotel.

Gloria Nugent was a musician with a life of her own when she met the hard-drinking actor, before he'd left for New York. She had recently been through a messy divorce and had no desire to get involved. But she saw how vulnerable he was, and she felt protective of him. Jack and Gloria lived together on and off for short periods of time, until the situation became impossible. She left on several occasions, but invariably she returned.

"I hate to see human beings with talent destroying themselves," she explained. "I saw people making a fool of him in The George, using him as a jester. Jack would get drunk and he would be very funny. Then he would drink too much and he would perhaps get very difficult; the people drinking with him would just go off and leave him.

"To see what this man could do on stage and then see what was happening in his private life, it seemed so terrible. I didn't really want to get caught up with anyone then. But he was such a beautiful, worthwhile person, I finally made the choice to give up my life for his."

MacGowran's first stage assignment following *Juno* was Alun Owen's drama, *The Rough and Ready Lot*. Jack won high praise for his portrayal of Captain Kelly, a mercenary caught up in a South American revolution. But MacGowran himself was caught up with the work of Samuel Beckett during the run of the play.

If Jack had been unhappy about his performance in the Royal Court *Endgame*, Beckett was enamored of his acting. As a result, he created a new play especially with MacGowran's unique talents in mind, an uncompromising radio drama composed of sounds and silences called *Embers*. Donald McWhinnie, whose imaginative production of *All That Fall* had met with Beckett's approval, again directed; the new play was heard over BBC Third Programme on June 24, 1959.

Embers was Beckett's most claustrophobic theatrical experiment to date:

> The confines of the drama are the limits of one human skull, and the action is built from prolonged meditations of an old man withdrawn so deeply into himself that the surrounding world scarcely exists.
> — *The Times*, June 25, 1959

MacGowran played a man wandering on a deserted beach, talking incessantly to drown out the sound of the sea. Preoccupied with the past, the guilt-ridden Henry talks to the ghost of his father, cursing the act of procreation that brought him into the world ("Washout... Wish to Christ she had") and reminisces about his and his wife's struggle to conceive their own child — which he also regrets.

Neither MacGowran nor Beckett regretted *Embers*, which won the Prix Italia prize that fall. MacGowran gave the most memorable of all his performances on radio, employing a voice that ranged from a soft croon to an hysterical rasp. Yet he was perhaps out of his element in a medium where he could be heard but not seen.

With Alan Dobie in *The Rough and Ready Lot*. London, 1959.

"He could do anything verbally, but you really had to see him to appreciate what he could do," asserted Patrick Magee, who did many radio plays with MacGowran, including *All That Fall* and *Embers*. "You had to *see* Jackie, the way he moved, the way he walked. He had a marvelous physical capability; he could collapse before your very eyes. One minute he was standing up and the next minute he was — collapsed."

By July, MacGowran was in rehearsals for a new musical, his second that year. Peter Wildebloode's tale of the Soho underworld gave him the starring role of Jug Ears — the leader of an inept gang of crooks — and his name in lights for the first time. But his first glimpse of the marquee was crushing:

JACK McGOWRAN IN *THE CROOKED MILE*

The show was a "smash" when it opened at the Cambridge Theatre in London's West End that fall; its star was often smashed during the run, at times with good reason. A few days after the première, an old schoolmate came backstage. "You've got your name up in lights and everything," he raved. The man asked for his autograph on a piece of paper.

"Oh, no," said Jack, "you don't want my autograph." The man insisted until he got it. Suddenly his look changed from one of affection to one of hatred; he tore the autograph in little pieces and walked out. Jack and Gloria were shattered; they took refuge in the stage door pub.

Elisabeth Welch, who co-starred with MacGowran, recalled another evening he came in "tight." The were doing a scene together in the first act when a patron in a box seat yelled, "That man's pissed!"

"It wasn't very loud," said Welch, "but the orchestra heard it, and we heard it. To Jack it had the effect of being splashed with cold water. He tried to pull himself together and get through it. Then he did his song and he was unsteady on his feet; he looked like an electric puppet that had been shorted out. But Jackie was theatre, if ever anybody was theatre. He was *magic*."

A precocious young director who was about to take over the Shakespeare Memorial Theatre — and forge something of a legend for himself in the process — had stopped by to have a look at the show during its pre-West End tryout in Liverpool. Peter Hall decided that MacGowran had "the perfect qualities for a Shakespearean clown" and invited him to join what would soon be renamed the Royal Shakespeare Company. The salary wasn't much, but the role of Feste in *Twelfth Night* was a plum Jack couldn't pass up.

The Crooked Mile closed after six months and Jack took a week off before going up to Stratford to play comic relief for the 1960 season. He went down to Devon to visit Sean O'Casey, who advised him to reconsider. "The secondary clowns are awful parts and you'll drink yourself to death," warned O'Casey. "I wouldn't do that if I were you."

MacGowran thought it would be a great experience to work with the prestigious repertory company, but when he got to Stratford, he learned that veteran actor Max Adrian had been signed to play Feste far in advance. Jack found himself cast in the meager roles of Autolycus, Speed, Christopher Sly and Old Gobbo.

"It's a pity Jack didn't get any good parts at Stratford," said Peter O'Toole, who played Shylock and Petruchio that season. "There was a great deal he could've brought to Shakespeare. There are many roles people don't touch he could have skated."

For all the problems that plagued the Broadway production of *Juno*, there was no less chaos behind the scenes in Stratford. The actors were young and energetic: Denholm Elliott, Dorothy Tutin, Diana Rigg and Ian Holm were among the members of the company. But the all-too-obvious inexperience of 29- year-old Peter Hall, coupled with the vague intentions of young directors like John Barton, spelled disaster.

"They were undergraduates," recalled MacGowran, in an interview shortly before his death. "They were trying to give Shakespeare meaning he never had, like people reading into Beckett meaning he never had. We [the actors] were all trapped, all frustrated. The pub became the place to be anesthetized against problems."

Hall chose to inaugurate the season with his own production of the seldom-staged *The Two Gentlemen of Verona*. By most accounts it was a dull and unimaginative interpretation of what one critic called "Shakespeare's worst play." Unfortunately, it set the pattern for what Peter O'Toole later characterized as a "deeply depressing" season.

"We were all deeply unhappy, though we were doing very good work," said O'Toole. "We were drinking so much because we had to contend with Peter Hall. We had to suffer with that prick for nine months!"

MacGowran and O'Toole, along with many of the other players who had been lured up to Midlands, fell into a wild routine that was, in essence, one perpetual party and one collective hangover. The path between the stage door and the local pub, the Black Swan — which the actors nicknamed "The Dirty Duck" — became a regular and well-traveled route. If the performers were not always sober, they were generally conscientious; they were particularly fond of dunking each other in tubs of ice water to bring themselves around.

The actors kept themselves in high spirits in more ways than one, in spite of — and perhaps because of — their discontent with the productions. "We danced on tables, we played tennis and hurley in pantomime, without a ball, and had rugby matches too. We sprinted; we even stole punts and went sailing down the Avon at 3 a.m.," claimed O'Toole. "Once Jack accused me of getting him drunk to enter into a bet that he wouldn't drink." On another occasion he made Jack "one of my father's special cocktails: mustard, salt, two cigarettes..."

Some of the actor's offstage exploits have become the stuff of legend — notably the night MacGowran and O'Toole discovered themselves with no food and retired without supper. The next morning they allegedly found a plate with the backbones of their pet goldfish — King Lear and Cordelia — picked clean. They each accused the other of dropping the goldfish into a frying pan in a weak moment during the night — though neither would admit it.

When Hall threatened to fire MacGowran because of his drinking, Gloria promised to look after him. But she did not realize she was only compounding the problem of Jack's alcoholism by making excuses for him.

If MacGowran distinguished himself as Speed in the season's opener, in spite of Hall's direction, he found no challenge in playing the elderly Gobbo in *The Merchant of Venice*. He decided to alleviate boredom early in the game; if he was playing a blind man, he reasoned, why not play it *blind*? He kept his eyes closed throughout rehearsals and performances, refusing to open them even for curtain calls.

Jack amused himself by going on blind, but not blind drunk. "He was often drunk in Stratford, but he would never show it on stage," said Gloria. "There were times when he was paralytic. He went on and he was brilliant; when he came off he was drunk again."

When John Barton enlarged the role of Christopher Sly for Jack in *The Taming of the Shrew*, the actor was hopeful. But the director's overly academic approach to the play sabotaged the effort from the start. For openers, he decided to stage the sixteenth century curtain-raiser, *Ralph Roister Doister*, with MacGowran, Patrick Wymark and Frances Cuka doing a jig and jumping into a box.

Barton got so involved with the choreography that he spent his time rehearsing the prelude instead of the play. Jack's patience eventually wore thin. "I'm not doing it," he shouted one night, kicking the box across the stage. "I absolutely refuse to do it."

The Winter's Tale — the one remaining chance to do something worthwhile — ultimately proved to be the final humiliation of the season. Peter Wood's production was inventive to the point of being ludicrous. "How is Autolycus supposed to enter with a harpsichord?!" MacGowran demanded to know.

Gloria Nugent had arrived at a turning point in her own frustrations by this time. *Jack's got to be able to stop drinking,* she thought to herself. One night she decided to show him what it was like when other people drank as much as he did; she took a bottle of brandy and drank it straight down. The stunt shook Jack sober. But Gloria failed to understand that Jack's drinking was a chronic problem, one she could not cure that easily; she walked out on him several times.

The actor never thought about the effect of his drinking on other people. He admired a man like Jimmy O'Dea, who never got drunk when important people were around. MacGowran would down every drink put into his hand at a party or a reception; O'Dea cleverly poured his into the planters.

MacGowran found it hard to cope with the injustices life heaped upon him; he was too delicate a man to survive the often cruel exigencies of his chosen profession. Like Brendan Behan and Dylan Thomas,

As Trinculo, another of Shakespeare's clowns, in a TV production of *The Tempest*.

he possessed a bit too much sensitivity for the world in which he lived. Mendacity angered him; incompetence drove him to the end of his tether, and Stratford served up both in unhealthy proportions.

6

He drank not wisely but too well. That the liquor was livelier than the muse, there was no question. As MacGowran sought to liberate himself from the pain of his existence — the lack of work, the stereotypical attitudes of producers and directors, the problems in New York and Stratford — he alienated most all his friends, discouraged potential employers and very nearly rationalized his way into the grave.

MacGowran had a tendency to say things when he was drunk he should have said when he was sober. He kept his anger bottled up inside; when he was intoxicated, the hostility came pouring out. In Stratford, he would call Peter Hall at 4 a.m. and say things he should have said during rehearsal.

When he was out of work, he didn't know who to blame. He now spoke much more lucidly; his theatrical diction had developed to where people were scarcely aware of his roughhewn Dublin patois. But neither accident of nationality nor physical limitations were any longer at fault; MacGowran had principally himself to blame for being unemployable.

At times he floundered in despair. But his dark moods were not always apparent; he often disguised his melancholia with a boisterous gaiety. MacGowran could bring the dullest party to life. Someone would say, "Be the fat man," and he would *be* the fat man; "Be the thin man" and he became the thin man. He also liked to tell the story about two Englishmen in a lavatory:

"Pardon me. Can you tell me the way to Oldham?"

"Some 'old 'em this way, some 'old 'em that way, and some just let 'em hang."

The gag developed into a pantomime that became a party favorite — impressions of different men in a urinal and their various styles of passing water. One night, at a New Year's Eve party in Chelsea, the band took a break and Jack's pals told him to get up and do the routine. The musicians had all cleared out, except for the burly black drummer standing against the wall. Suddenly there was a splashing sound, and Jack was urinating into the drum.

To his drinking buddies, it was hysterically funny. But others, who saw MacGowran destroying himself with the booze, were saddened by his unpredictable behavior. The actor himself was blissfully unaware of his actions, and rarely was he confronted with them.

When the 1960 season ended in Stratford, Jack returned to London feeling poor and drained. He went to see a physician, but he was unprepared for the advice he received. "I'll give you five months if you keep drinking," the doctor warned. "You've done a lot of damage to yourself. If you want to live you'll quit now."

MacGowran went back to his flat in a state of depression. He decided he needed a drink to bolster his courage and took a bottle of whiskey from the cabinet. Then he had second thoughts and emptied the bottle in the sink.

Learning to live without alcohol was a torturous ordeal. "It was like a death," said Gloria MacGowran. "I was there but it was his decision." For three months Jack lay in bed with his face against the wall. For a man who loved drinking and being with people, the fun and the laughter and the songs — a man who hesitated to go to the bathroom for fear he would miss something — it was almost too difficult to quit.

Whether touring the wine cellars of Paris with John Wayne, carousing in Mexico with Pedro Armendariz or getting liquidated with Trevor Howard in Spain — where they were robbed by the police — MacGowran felt he could hold his own in any company. But the doctor's ultimatum forced him to admit that his body had taken all the punishment it could endure.

After a period of abstinence Jack began to feel better. He began drawing and writing poetry, and he started to enjoy life. With Gloria's help, he then attempted to resuscitate his career; he had acquired a reputation for being unreliable and it was not easy to get back into the business.

MacGowran's appearance in a number of low-budget horror films and melodramas — and his lack of visibility on the London stage — attest sharply to the fact that the early sixties were lean years. The BBC television production of *Waiting for Godot* was one of his few worthwhile endeavors in 1961.

Samuel Beckett had authored the play destined to become the most widely analyzed and discussed of the twentieth century a dozen years earlier, as a diversion "from the awful prose I was writing at the time." To his dismay, it would become far more successful than the novels he considered to be his more important work.

MacGowran starred in the TV adaptation with Peter Woodthorpe — who reprised his role from the first London stage production — as Vladimir and Estragon, the forlorn tramps who wait in vain for the

Jack MacGowran and Peter Woodthorpe, as Vladimir and Estragon, in the 1961 TV adaptation of *Waiting for Godot*.

mysterious Godot, making conversation to pass the time, seeking something to give them the impression they exist.

Donald McWhinnie rehearsed the production as a stage play; in a daring experiment, he followed the action with a single camera and did no cutting. Much of the play was photographed in tight close-ups, emphasizing the claustrophobic element. It was a bold, imaginative stroke, but the director was dissatisfied.

"Jackie was excellent, but the play didn't work on television," said McWhinnie. "I don't think it can. When you put *Waiting for Godot* on the small screen it loses the artificiality; it's too realistic. We tried to give it some kind of stylization by doing it all with one camera. Beckett wasn't too happy about it."

Jack won the British Television Actor of the Year award for his performance nonetheless. Observed poet-critic Louis MacNeice:

> MacGowran's tragi-comic face face (a blend of Teniel's Mad Hatter, Harpo Marx and the less stupid peasants of Brueghel) is such a natural on the screen that it is unfair to anyone he is playing with.
> — *The New Statesman*, July 7, 1961

During the TV taping, MacGowran commuted back and forth between London and Bristol, where he was appearing nightly in Eugène Ionesco's *The Killer*. The Ionesco play, with its bizarre plot and absurd dialogue, was no more welcome in its British première than *Godot* had been; *The Killer*, however, proved far less durable.

MacGowran had become acquainted with Ionesco's work in 1957, shortly after his introduction to Beckett; in the title role of a "gallant but almost incomprehensible" production of *Amédée*, he was an uninspired playwright with a problem on his hands: how to get rid of a corpse.

The actor had initiated a friendship with the Roumanian-born playwright while he was in Paris visiting Beckett. Ionesco was having trouble getting his work produced at the time; through an interpreter, he told Jack he was dissatisfied with his agents, and asked him to handle his plays.

Jack's attempts to restage the surreal *Amédée* in London failed to come to fruition, as did a South African tour of *The Chairs*. His efforts to revive *The Killer* following the Bristol Old Vic production were equally unsuccessful, despite the playwright's encouragement.

MacGowran admired Ionesco for his angle on life, but acting in his plays did not give Jack near the satisfaction he derived from doing Beckett. "All the best plays he has written are one-act plays, but he knows they are hard to sell, so he pads them into three acts. There was a lot of unnecessary material in *The Killer*," said MacGowran. "Whereas on the other hand you have Beckett, who has brought everything down to a minimum, you read Ionesco adding on stuff."

Jack was still persona non grata on the London stage when he played Drinkwater, the Cockney, in a 1962 production of *Captain Brassbound's Conversion* in Croyden, Surrey. A drama critic who was otherwise unimpressed with the play felt the actor "produced enough pathos to force a revision of long-held opinion about Shaw's ignorance of the working class." That fall, Jack would force theatregoers and critics alike to look at Beckett in a different light.

When MacGowran was asked to do something for the Dublin Theatre Festival, a one-man show based on the work of Beckett was not the first project that came to mind. Nor was it Jack's idea. Only when his attempts to resurrect *In Sand* once again fell through did Gloria suggest an anthology of sorts, derived from Beckett's novels and plays.

The concept appealed immediately to MacGowran, but not in the manner she had intended. "My idea was to change people's ideas about Jack, to show the different facets of things he could do. We chose things that would show the range he had. It was a totally selfish thing on my part," recalled Gloria MacGowran. "But Jack wanted to show the beauty and the humor in Sam; that was his concern."

MacGowran called Beckett and asked for his approval, then went to Paris to discuss the project. Beckett was delighted with the idea. Jack chose *Act Without Words I*, the author's elaborate "mime for one player," as a basic framework. He also selected a long, convoluted monologue from *Waiting for Godot*; a speech from *Endgame*; an excerpt from the seminal novel, *Molloy*; a poetic passage from the radio play, *All That Fall*; an erotic reminiscence of a girl in a boat from *Krapp's Last Tape*; and the short prose piece, *From an Abandoned Work*, in its entirety.

Sean Kenny designed an appropriately barren set, including the leafless tree from *Godot*, and Donald McWhinnie agreed to direct. Background music was supplied by a recording of Miles Davis' understated jazz trumpet solo, "Blue in Green." Alluding to Beckett's preoccupation with nightfall, Jack called the program *End of Day*.

MacGowran and McWhinnie rehearsed the show on an irregular basis, inbetween jobs, "an hour here, an hour there, over a period of months," recalled the director. "Artistically it wasn't really satisfactory. Jack didn't have the texts down, he hadn't mastered the words; he felt he was dedicated to Sam's work at the time, but he hadn't quite... gradually he came around to an awareness of things.

"The project wasn't too well conceived, but it was a kind of starting point. It needed a lot more thought and working out," said

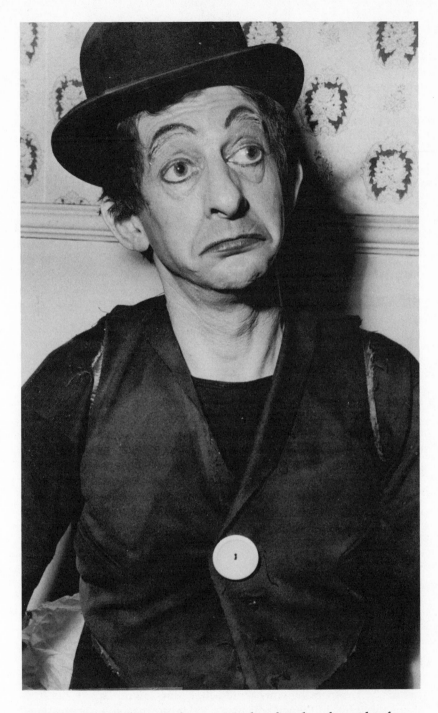

In costume for *End of Day*, his first one-man how based on the works of
Beckett. Dublin, 1962.

McWhinnie. "The great thing about working with Jack is that you didn't have to be terribly tactful, as with some performers, and play to their ego — you could be absolutely honest with him and say, 'Jackie, that's terrible.' He didn't mind being told."

MacGowran's lone, black-clad bowler-hatted figure was the hit of the theatre festival when *End of Day* premièred in Dublin on October 5, 1962. The Gaiety Theatre was filled to capacity for his one-night stand. "Mr. MacGowran demolished once and for all the caricature of Beckett as a gloomy, obscure dramatist of dustbins, deformity and despair," declared Alec Reid in *The Irish Times*.

The Royal Court made a bid to transfer the show to London as a companion piece to Beckett's *Happy Days*, which was being mounted with the author's supervision. Instead, *End of Day* transferred to the New Arts Theatre Club, in a late-night time slot where it did not always draw an appreciative audience.

MacGowran's decision to depart from the pantomime, speaking passages of text and then returning to it, aroused much controversy. While *Punch* observed that it was not unlike "a tasting of great wines in a friendly cellar," *The Times* critic felt the combination could only have been pulled off by an English-speaking Jean-Louis Barrault.

"There are very few things in London I would hate more to have missed," commented drama critic Tom Stoppard, who was reminded of Chaplin. The future playwright had no quarrel with the show's format:

> At first there is something too arbitrary about assembling what is virtually a new bastard play by channeling speeches from eight sources into one character. But it works because Beckett's view of man's estate is consistent in all of them, a look of pity and ironic amusement, the exact opposite of laughing till one cries — crying till one laughs.
>
> — *Scene*, October 25, 1962

Beckett had seen the show in rehearsal but had no input on the script. While he was generally pleased with the result, he was unhappy with the way MacGowran had used the pantomime. "Sam didn't say 'Don't do it,' but the very fact that he'd clouded his face Jack knew — he clearly wasn't happy about it," said Gloria MacGowran.

Beckett gently told the actor, "A mime is served best without words." To others he commented that MacGowran spoke his lines "exactly right," but reportedly described the format as "an aberration." Jack had to admit that the juxtaposition of mime and speech didn't work — but then this was only a makeshift that could not long content a man like MacGowran.

If the show was not entirely satisfactory, it proved that Jack could do almost anything. No one was more convinced than Beckett, who decided to write a challenging new stage piece for him. *J.M. Mime* began with a series of elaborate mathematical computations that would manipulate the actor to and fro, along all the possible paths in a complex geometrical pattern plotted on the stage; it was in some ways the most complicated exercise Beckett had yet written for the theatre. However, he eventually abandoned the project.

When MacGowran was asked to film the earlier Beckett pantomimes, *Act Without Words I* and *II*, and the monologue from *Waiting for Godot* in a package for Irish television, he dismissed the idea. However, he agreed to do the first of the two mimes — sans words, as Beckett intended — when director Jim Fitzgerald managed to obtain the rights for £17.50.

Act Without Words I was far from simple, but much less severe than the concept for *J.M. Mime*. The script called for MacGowran to be flung about the stage and tantalized by objects just outside his reach; his puppet-like character's every effort, including suicide, was doomed to failure. MacGowran rehearsed and filmed the Beckett pantomime in one grueling 16-hour day — despite the intense physical demands of the piece — at his own insistence.

Meanwhile the actor received a number of offers to tour Europe and the United States with *End of Day*. Initially he was delighted, but as an ever- increasing number of promoters became involved, he turned down all bids. "He didn't like the people who were making the offers," asserted Gloria. "They appeared to be hustlers. He got other offers later on, but again, he didn't like the terms and he didn't like the people."

He was not sorry he accepted Tony Richardson's offer to appear in *Tom Jones*, even though the film interrupted rehearsals for *End of Day*. MacGowran's appearance in this bawdy, Academy Award-winning farce — as the highwayman who tries to rob Albert Finney on the road to London and turns out to be his long-lost "father" — did much to bolster his reputation.

From the outset, director Richardson felt his real work was in the casting; once he found the right actors, he had only to turn them loose. "Jackie's great strength was in his personality, his ability to draw you into his world. He was the perfect choice for the role of Partridge," said Richardson, who filled his cast with actors from the Royal Court Theatre. "Jackie was like a unique instrument — not an instrument that would usually be part of an orchestra, but one that had a particular

With Albert Finney in *Tom Jones*, which won four Academy Awards and brought them both to the attention of a wider public.

quality to it, like a psaltery. He was like an instrument that you would use on a special occasion."

Few directors had such respect for MacGowran in those days. He appeared in a number of films during the early sixties, but most were unexceptional. Jack did films only because he had to eat, and he was generally choosy about the roles. Some, however, were accidents.

When José Ferrer called from Italy and invited Jack over for "a bit of a holiday," he happily accepted. He had finished his run at the New Arts performing *End of Day* to half-empty houses, and a vacation was in order. He wasn't there long, however, when he found himself at work.

Ferrer was filming something called *Cyrano et D'Artagnan* for Abel Gance. The day after Jack arrived in Terrania, he was told, "Gance wants to see you." The director handed MacGowran a page of dialogue and asked him to recite it; the next thing he knew, he was playing Scaramouche.

Because he admired the French film pioneer, who was best known for the silent epic, *Napoleon*, MacGowran did the picture for practically nothing. But it was only a tiny part and he didn't want to use his real name. Taking the literal meaning of his name from the Irish — "son of summer" — he whimsically translated it into Italian, calling himself Giovanni de l'Estate.

The actor in MacGowran would have relished the part of Cyrano; privately, the man was ever sensitive about his own nose. Jack never pictured himself as a leading man type — he knew his scope — but he had never forgotten Ernest Blythe's remark about the size of his proboscis. That year Jack went to see a plastic surgeon in Oxford. The doctor, however, refused to alter his appearance. "I think you've got a great nose," he said.

Peter O'Toole, who had gotten a nose job himself for *Lawrence of Arabia* and become a star since their days in Stratford, was fond of boasting that doors were open for him that would never open for MacGowran. The diminutive actor had his detractors, and they were many, but he also had his champions.

Laurence Harvey was proud to be counted among the latter. MacGowran had been told Harvey was difficult to work with, when the actor-director first asked him to play a priest in *The Ceremony*. The warning had no basis in fact; Harvey took such a liking to him that he allowed his admiration for Jack's performance to interfere with the editing.

When MacGowran suggested his own part be trimmed for the benefit of the overall film, Harvey rejected his advice. Jack often found his scenes snipped and shredded in hands less appreciative of his abilities. The injustice of having his scenes deleted when they should have been left in — and having them run on when they should have been cut — distressed him no end.

Richard Brooks' *Lord Jim* offered MacGowran a prominent role on paper — as the engineer of a ship cowardly deserted in a storm — but the picture proved only a disappointment. Jack spent two difficult weeks shooting the storm sequence in a tank at Shepperton Studios, with nothing to show for it; only a glimpse of the scene remained in the film.

The pleasures of cavorting with Peter O'Toole on location in Hong Kong and Cambodia were slim consolation. As in Stratford, they spent their time making merry and mischief, but the memory of their off-screen diversions did little to alleviate Jack's anguish at the final product. "It upset him to put himself into something and then for there to be so little left when it came out," said Gloria MacGowran.

"When a role was offered to him and there were scenes with the stars, he was very pleased. After many films he found out that if you have a scene with the star, and you attract more attention than he does, you end up on the cutting room floor. After *Lord Jim*, Jack said, 'I'll never do another film where I have anything to say to the star."

MacGowran did not take his own dictum seriously, but there were times when he was content to let the star do all the talking. When the star was Burgess Meredith, and the vehicle was Eugene O'Neill's intimate two-character one-act, *Hughie*, he was especially pleased.

Meredith played the compulsive talker, Erie Smith, in the 1963 Bath Theatre Festival production, opposite MacGowran as the terminally-bored night clerk of a rundown hotel. MacGowran was sitting motionless behind the hotel desk in his near-mute role one evening, when he moved suddenly and got a laugh. Meredith screamed his line and turned around. *That was a mistake*, thought Jack. *I'll never move again.*

"*Hughie* is difficult to perform," observed Meredith. "If the clerk gets too pantomimic, nobody can understand what's going on; it becomes a two- ring circus. Jackie had to do it in gentle terms, but come out of it to speak once in a while. If the night clerk wants to, he can throw the whole thing. I was always grateful that Jackie was was merciful in that, most sensitive and introspective."

To Meredith's regret, *Hughie* had been packaged with "two bad O'Neill one-acts." Worse yet, he was saddled with the role of master of ceremonies — despite the fact that he was ill — introducing the plays and linking them together with "some sort of sappy narrative" that served no real purpose.

On location with Peter O'Toole in *Lord Jim*.

"The things that happened were unbelievable. It was a complete amateur set-up," recalled Meredith. "The leading lady went wild just before opening night, screaming and yelling in some sort of private fantasy. It nearly drove me out of my mind. One night the candelabra kept falling down, whenever I started to speak.

"Through it all, Jackie was very solid and very helpful. With all his basically neurotic soul, he had a toughness to him that could withstand the knocks. Our one experience on stage together was not that spectacular, but it was eventful in that it cemented a friendship."

It was also during *Hughie* that MacGowran finally cemented his relationship with Gloria Nugent. On March 21, 1963, they said their vows before a justice of the peace in Westminster, with Peter O'Toole present as best man. If their honeymoon was preempted by rehearsals for the play, Gloria was the only woman in a long line of girlfriends and fiancées who managed to get MacGowran to the altar. The "digging years" appeared to be at an end, and marriage was no longer the frightening proposition it had once been. The theatre would remain his mistress, but not his only love.

At an Irish tennis match with his wife, Gloria. 1970.

Gloria, who then had two teenage daughters by her first marriage, soon decided that having a child "would be good for Jack." He became a father for the first and only time, at 46, when Gloria gave birth to Tara late the following year.

The proud mother jubilantly rang friends with the news: "You'll die yourself laughing," she said.

"What do you mean?" they responded.

"It's a girl," announced Gloria, "and she's the image of Jackie."

7

In the year that followed MacGowran's first attempt at putting together a one-man show, he began to develop a far deeper appreciation of Samuel Beckett's spare and elusive work. Jack and Sam met on several occasions in the spring of 1963, while the actor was directing W.B. Yeats' *The Countess Cathleen* for the Paris Festival.

MacGowran and Beckett talked less about Sam's work, or Jack's, than they did about Dublin. Beckett had much the same obsession with Dublin as Joyce. He enjoyed talking about Dublin characters and people he knew; he cared little for conversations that centered on his writing, or himself. But as their alliance grew, MacGowran decided that he could no longer act in anything of Beckett's without the man's supervision. Sam, for his part, began to regard Jack as his personal emissary.

Unable to go to Dublin for the Irish première of his new play, *Happy Days*, in the fall of 1963 — and worried about the presentation — Beckett asked the actor to take a look at the show and report back to him. John Beary's production was one of the highlights of the theatre festival, and received unusually good notices. But when the play moved to the East End of London in December, MacGowran took over as director — again, at Beckett's request.

Unlike Beckett's previous plays, this one was a tour-de-force for a woman — a fat, middle-aged woman at first imbedded up to her waist in a mound of earth, and in the second act buried up to her neck. Jack's imagination was spurred by the character of the relentlessly optimistic Winnie. "Sam," he said afterwards, "I'd love to play *Happy Days* in drag."

Beckett was highly amused by the suggestion, though it never came to fruition. He was not amused, however, by the suggestions of other actors, with which he was being inundated. When Peter O'Toole expressed a desire to produce and star in a film of *Waiting for Godot*, the author turned him down. O'Toole had already publicized his plans to make the picture on a two-week shooting schedule in the west of Ireland, on a budget of £20,000 — and put Tom Stoppard to work on a screenplay — but the answer was still no.

MacGowran, who was to have played Lucky in O'Toole's film, had himself talked to Beckett at great length about putting *Godot* on screen.

But the playwright gently refused to yield. Beckett had already begun to make it known that he did not want his works done in any medium other than the ones for which they were deliberately written. He had made and would continue to make exceptions; he had grudgingly allowed *Godot* to be produced on television, where it remained theatrical, but decided it could not possibly survive transition to the big screen. "How can you photograph words?" he protested.

Instead of compromising his work, Beckett surprised MacGowran by writing a new work with the actor in mind, a script for a silent movie. *Film* was designed specifically *for* the cinema, unlike anything else the author had written.

The plot was simple, the theme complex: the camera would relentlessly pursue MacGowran as he tried to escape from watching eyes, human, animal, inanimate; ultimately, "O" escapes from everyone and everything, except himself. As summarized by Beckett: "one striving to see one striving not to be seen."

Alan Schneider, who had staged the American premières of Beckett's plays, was chosen to direct the project. His inability to deal with various production problems caused a succession of foul-ups and delays; he eventually got *Film* off the ground, six weeks behind schedule. But by then MacGowran was committed to the Royal Shakespeare production of *Endgame* and could not free himself to do the picture. Buster Keaton — a favorite of Beckett's, as well as MacGowran's — was selected in Jack's place.

MacGowran was distressed that he was unable to do the film; Beckett, however, would soon assuage his disappointment by writing something else especially for him. He kept Jack in mind whenever one of his plays was being staged, and recommended the earnest actor to directors.

A few months earlier, when Beckett had casually mentioned that a group of amateur actors were planning to stage an English-language *Endgame* in Paris, he did not think MacGowran would be interested. But the memory of the 1958 production rankled, and Jack welcomed to opportunity to improve on his portrayal of Clov; he had made several attempts to revive the play himself in London, to no avail.

This time MacGowran was determined to have a suitable stage partner. His longtime friend, Patrick Magee, was the ideal choice. A native of Northern Ireland, Magee had begun a fruitful association with Beckett seven years earlier, alongside MacGowran in the BBC broadcast of *All That Fall*. Beckett, impressed by the actor's deep, resonant voice, then wrote *Krapp's Last Tape* especially for him.

Magee's agent did not want the actor to go to Paris. There was little

Patrick Magee in Beckett's *Krapp's Last Tape.*

money in the job and he felt it was of no consequence. "Nobody will hear of it," he protested. MacGowran talked Magee into playing Hamm against his agent's wishes, much to Beckett's delight.

Hamm and Clov, as conceived by Beckett, were two of the most physically-demanding roles ever written for actors. The blind, autocratic Hamm, who barks orders from his wheelchair throne, and the stiff-legged Clov, who resentfully obeys his commands, required highly-defined skills: Magee's Hamm would draw its immense authority from the vocal versatility he had cultivated while touring the Irish provinces; MacGowran's Clov, no less contorted than Olivier's Richard III, would make optimum use of the muscular coordination he had acquired on Dublin's athletic fields.

"There was a perfect balance between Jack and Pat," said composer Edward Beckett, the playwright's nephew. "Sam would do things for them he wouldn't do for anyone else. He knew he could get them to do it the way it was supposed to be — he was pleased to find someone like Jack who wouldn't do something 'creative' with the material."

From the gaming room of a nightclub to a flat over a pub, MacGowran and Magee shuffled between one location and another for five weeks of rehearsal in London. Edward Albee and Harold Pinter, both heavily influenced by Beckett in their own writing, were two of many casual visitors during rehearsal.

The production got off to a shaky start when the young director, Michael Blake, proved inadequate. Beckett, who had intended only to supervise, ending up directing the production while Blake stood in the background; he refused, however, to take credit on the program. His direction itself was tentative.

"The work atmosphere was always quiet, curiously formal, even delicate, often intense," noted journalist Clancy Sigal, whose day-by-day account of the rehearsal period provided Londoners with an intimate glimpse of Beckett at work:

> As the players run through their lines Beckett pores over the text as though hearing it for the first time. He glares sharply, neutrally, at the action... "A little more pause there." A grainy, almost silent voice, a courteous Irish lilt and lisp, with a repressed, lean bark. Leanness is the chief, the central characteristic of this man... He is both decisive and terribly afraid of giving offence to the actors.
> — *The Sunday Times Magazine*, March 1, 1964

While Beckett *was* afraid the actors would be offended at his suggestions, they enthusiastically welcomed his input. MacGowran, having suffered through George Devine's production six years earlier — at a time when Beckett was far more hesitant about putting himself forward — was delighted. "Some day we must do this properly," he had told Beckett; the time had finally come.

MacGowran now understood what the play was really about: "No man is an island. Hamm is helpless without Clov to wheel him around and tell him what's happening. Clov has no one else; he's afraid to face this barren waste of world outside. It's a picture of two people totally dependent on each other, and really hating each other at the same time. But loving each other too; one would miss the other desperately."

Magee was equally enlightened: "Clov is Hamm's eyes. Hamm is the mind, Clov's the body. It's like Vladimir and Estragon in *Waiting for Godot* — they're two halves of the same person. What seems to escape people is that the work's very funny — terrifying, but very funny as well."

The possibilities for humor did not escape Beckett, who had insisted on no comedy at all in the first production. "Let's get as many laughs as we can out of this horrible mess," he instructed the cast this time out.

Neither Beckett nor the actors began with any preconceived notions. "The way to do *Endgame*, from my experience, is to forget totally any underlying profundity which may be in it," said Magee. "Sam directed us to play it as simply as possible, just to play the line for its own value."

As his reserve gave way, the author's attention to gesture and inflection became every bit as painstaking as the stage directions he had set forth on paper. His ear for pronunciation was as sharp as his sense of humor:

Clov:	I can't sit.
Hamm:	True. And I can't stand.
Clov:	So it is.
Hamm:	Every man his speci*al*ity.

"Sam doesn't actually 'direct' in that sense of the word," asserted Pat Magee. "He would just watch us do it and then we'd ask him, 'What the hell's it mean? What are you getting at here?' And Sam would quite lucidly and simply tell us. He's like Joyce — there's never a word he can't justify. No sloppy carelessness; everything is absolutely down the line."

In one scene, Magee-Hamm instructed MacGowran-Clov to look out the window:

Hamm:	And the sun?
Clov:	Zero.
Hamm:	But it should be sinking. Look again.

"What on God's earth does that mean?" Magee asked the playwright.

"Well," said Beckett, "you see the kind of fellow Hamm is, he loves things coming to an end, but he doesn't really want them *to* end."

Beckett placed few restrictions on the imagination of his actors. "I only know what's on the page," he amiably told the cast. "Do it your way." He paid no attention to the larger implications of the play, and instructed the actors not to look for symbols in his work. As writer Sigal further noted:

His interventions are almost always not on the side of subtlety but of simplicity... The actors tend to want to make the play abstract and "existential"; gently and firmly Beckett guides them to concrete, exact and simple actions.

"If you are lost as to what to do, he will tell you that he would like a move made in that direction and the head held a certain way," MacGowran observed. "But he allows any amount of freedom, provided he feels it doesn't conflict with the text."

Beckett was far more at home in the theatre than he had been at the time of the Royal Court production. If the playwright was still a little apprehensive about directing, he surprised the cast by trimming a number of lines and cutting everything he felt was of "a purely literary value."

Endgame opened in Paris on February 18, 1964, to the sort of reception MacGowran had always hoped for, playing to packed houses throughout its run. The play that had once driven audiences from the theatre ended its run being performed for crowds that refused to leave — until the actors came back, and sat down to discuss the show with them.

The claustrophobic 250-seat Studio des Champs-Élysées — where Roger Blin had staged *Fin de partie* — was an artistic choice in itself. "It was exactly the right size, the right shape," enthused Magee. "It was like a tunnel."

His every move precisely calculated as he skittered about the stage, his delivery toneless and drained of emotion, MacGowran's Clov was a characterization honed to perfection, "a white-faced clown... whose limbs wreathed like plant stems seeking the light," observed one critic. Noted *The Times*:

[His] Clov has grown from the mole-like passivity of his 1958 performance to a state of grotesque muscular contortion which excruciatingly intensifies his actions as a slave, painfully clambering up a ladder to view the landscape and shuffling on with flailing arms at the summons of Hamm's dog whistle.

"Jackie had the most extraordinary affinity for Beckett's work," said Magee. "Something in him latched on to it. Someone came around after the play — someone interested in acting — and asked him, how did he do it. Jackie said, 'I don't know how to do it — I just do it.' He had no theory; he made up the character and presented it. Simple as that. Jackie knew exactly what he was doing all the time; he was enormously

Pat Magee and Jack MacGowran, as Hamm and Clov, rehearsing for the first Beckett-directed *Endgame*. London, 1964.

instinctive. On stage it was back and forth between us, like a marvelous tennis match."

MacGowran was not always happy in a team situation. Actors who were not wholly dedicated to their work infuriated him; poor timing — particularly in a Beckett play — drove him mad. That Magee's Hamm was the perfect complement to his Clov was not lost on the critics:

> Pat Magee and Jack MacGowran work together like old, slightly putrid pub pals. They are consistently alert to each other's moods and project a relationship which is a mixture of reluctant affection and sullen dependence, seasoned with some coarse guffaws at life. They are King Lear and the Fool in a bad way in a dosshouse by the Liffey.
> — *The Guardian*, February 21, 1964

The landmark Paris *Endgame* proved to be the turning point in Magee's career. By the time the Royal Shakespeare Company imported the show, the demand for his talents was so great the 40-year-old actor found himself doing three plays at once; he portrayed the Marquis de Sade in Peter Brook's production of *Marat/Sade* and appeared in Pinter's *The Birthday Party*, in repertory with *Endgame* at the Aldwych Theatre.

Magee was worried about getting mixed up. If he went the wrong way in the Beckett, he could easily skip five pages. He had a terrible feeling he would miss something, he told MacGowran. "You're safe, old scout. I know it backwards," Jack assured him.

"Several times during the course of the show Hamm says to Clov, 'Be off.' Most of the time he doesn't go, there's another line. One time I said 'Be off,'" recalled Magee, "and off he went. I glanced into the wings, and there's Jackie looking at the script, and racing back on again. It was so easy to do in that play, so many questions and answers, 'Be off' and 'Come here' and so on — you could quite simply lose your way. Oddly enough, we almost never did."

The drama critic of *The Catholic Herald* felt MacGowran *had* lost his way, however. In his scathing "review" of the play, he attacked the actor for making himself "a sort of 'bishop' of the Beckett cult":

> In a programme note, [MacGowran] implies that the audience should find in *Endgame* a substitute for the liturgy — and if they haven't a liturgy they might adopt the scriptures according to Beckett. "It has given me," he solemnly proclaims, "an absolutely new sense of values." Absolutely new? One wonders what happened to Mr. MacGowran's old sense of values.

Theatregoers were considerably warmer in their reception, and many accepted MacGowran's invitation to join the "Beckett cult." One member of the audience swore his allegiance by leaving behind a program with a note scribbled in the margin: "Ah, yes, we see it all now: Sam Beckett is God, and Jackie MacGowran is his prophet!"

Donald McWhinnie, himself a tireless worker in the service of Beckett, restaged the play at the Aldwych in collaboration with the author. "I suppose we directed it together," asserted McWhinnie. "We were still asking him, 'What does this mean?' I worked in a very loose, freehand way — and Sam's function was to say, 'I don't know how to achieve the result — that's up to you... Is that the result? I don't like it.'

"The Aldwych was the wrong theatre for *Endgame*, too big; the Royal Court was ideal. But it was the right time for it. The audience found the humor in Beckett — it was a kind of revelation." Indeed, as *The Times* headline acknowledged:

An Early Failure is Now Almost a Riot

"It was a matter of time," said McWhinnie. "Everything matured. When Jackie played Clov in 1958, he used to sentimentalize it — there is always the temptation to put the Irish sentimentality into it, which is wrong. That first *Endgame* was really sentimental and sloppy and soft. Nobody quite knew in those days how to deal with this man Beckett."

Sean O'Casey was among those who could not deal with Beckett; he found little humor in his countryman's work and refused to join the growing cult. While both of MacGowran's favorite authors celebrated life in their writing, they were diametrically opposed to each other in philosophy.

"He isn't in me, nor am I in him," wrote O'Casey of Beckett. "I am not waiting for Godot to bring me life; I am out after life myself even at the age I've reached." MacGowran wanted to bring the two of them together, nonetheless, and Beckett was anxious to meet the elderly playwright. But O'Casey — who called *Waiting for Godot* "a rotting and remarkable play" — died on September 18, 1964, before a meeting could be arranged.

By December, MacGowran was in rehearsals for that "rotting and remarkable" play at the Royal Court — the third major London production of Beckett's work that year. *Waiting for Godot* had confused, bored and shocked Britain on its first appearance nine years earlier, and there were those who felt it was time for a new presentation.

"I had seen Peter Hall's original production in 1955, and I was struck by it. I thought it was an extraordinary piece of theatre," said director Anthony Page, who suggested a revival of *Godot* to Court artistic director George Devine. Beckett approved, and prepared a revised text for what would be the first unexpurgated version.

With Beckett in attendance during rehearsal, there was little confusion. "Everyone knew exactly what was intended with Sam around — it was all very real to him," asserted Page. "Sam had a very clear picture of the way it should be in his head, but he was very open-minded; he cut little things that weren't working. There was a lot of experimenting on *Godot*, trying things out. Beckett had the most energy of all of us; he never wanted to stop working."

Nicol Williamson, who was just beginning to make a name for himself, was cast as the long-suffering Vladimir — the role Jack had played so effectively on TV — while MacGowran took the part of Lucky, the woebegone slave. "Jackie was a classic piece of casting. We were lucky to get him," said Page. "He had an incredible insight into the character."

The insight was a long time coming, however. "When I first saw *Godot* [in 1955] I kept falling asleep and waking up and wondering what the hell was going on," MacGowran confessed. "I didn't understand a word of it, but I don't think the actors did either from the look and the sound of them."

Beckett's enigmatic tale of two derelicts awaiting a savior in the wilderness had been given many interpretations in the intervening years. But the true *Godot* — the one envisioned by Beckett — had been realized only once, in the author's opinion; not in Paris or New York or London, but in a German prison with convicts in the roles. "They understood that *Godot* is not despair, but hope," stated Beckett. "*Godot* is life — aimless, but always with an element of hope."

Beckett, who had disdained the many and varied analyses of the play that had been made over the years, felt invariably it was "a play that is striving all the time to avoid definition." Again, the simplest approach was the best. The obvious interpretations that even MacGowran ignored in the beginning were in fact correct.

"This is a play full of implications, and every important statement may be taken at three or four levels," Beckett acknowledged, in a rare comment to the press, during rehearsal for the 1964 production. "The actor has only to find the dominant one; because he does so does not mean the other levels will be lost."

As with *Endgame*, Beckett was tired of people looking for hidden meanings in his plays, and influences which did not exist. While comparisons had been made to dramas by Balzac, Strindberg and Yeats — all of which the author negated — Beckett had been largely

Photo by Zoë Dominic

Samuel Beckett shares a laugh with Jack MacGowran, during rehearsals for *Waiting for Godot*.

inspired by the two-reel comedies of Laurel and Hardy, of whom he was a great admirer.

MacGowran's part was more original and less like something suggested by a Laurel and Hardy film than anything else in the play. The shattered, emaciated Lucky was, in sum, "all life finally lived... a relic of all human decency at the mercy of the bourgeois," stated the actor. He was so named, said the playwright, because "he is Lucky to have no more expectations."

The role was one of great difficulty, and MacGowran sought Beckett's assistance early in rehearsal. The physical requirements of the part, to be played largely in mime, were comparatively easy for MacGowran — although the former athlete told a reporter it was "like running a four-minute mile twice in an evening." But Lucky's convoluted six-minute speech was another matter.

While MacGowran had an innate understanding of the Celtic rhythms in Beckett's work — along with the unmistakably Irish terrain — the disintegrating jumble of blasphemy and poetry that interrupts Lucky's silence in the first act seemed almost insurmountable at the outset. Indeed, the mad tirade had been the downfall of virtually every actor who had tackled the role.

The long, philosophical monologue, as MacGowran observed, is "an attempt to speak on the part of a man who was once a very accomplished speaker, one who knew fully how to explain about life, but who's now so senile and so overcome by circumstances that he has lost track of what he was going to say."

Beckett explained to him that the soliloquy was divided into three sections: the constancy of the divine — a personal God who "loves us dearly with some exceptions"; the shrinkage of humanity; and the petrifaction of the earth, the earth as an "abode of stones."

MacGowran convinced Beckett to record the monologue himself on tape, so that the actor could play it over and over, until he found the cadences of the the furious harangue. Jack slowed down the circuitous torrent of words so he could say them, speeding them up as he went along. As MacGowran-Lucky lost the focus of the speech, it became "a quick succession of words unrelated to each other" — but each and every syllable was clear and distinct. Jack never once altered or deleted a word, for each had a meaning, and a hue that varied the whole.

MacGowran *looked* every inch the "relic" of humanity Beckett had envisioned, from the rotting teeth and ghost-like complexion, to the funereal carriage of his skeletal frame. But there was far more to the characterization than mere externals, the stringy white hair or the gnarled rope about the neck. MacGowran's Lucky was man at the end of his tether, teetering on the brink of death. Jack had walked in Lucky's ruined shoes and he knew his agony; he understood Lucky's bewilderment and his pain in a way that Beckett could not — and need not — articulate.

Paul Curran, Nicol Williamson, Jack MacGowran and Alfred Lynch in the 1964 Royal Court production of *Waiting for Godot*.

8

Waiting for Godot played to packed houses during its revival at the Royal Court. Much had changed since the London première a decade earlier. "*Godot* is no longer experimental, provocative or potentially suspect," noted Alec Reid in *The Irish Times*. "For better or worse, it has attained the respectability of an established classic."

The play's author was delighted with the revival, which ran for nearly two months, and cheered by the reception; a simultaneous Berlin production, though well received, had been badly done. When Beckett wrote MacGowran to congratulate him on the reviews, he was typically concerned with the actor's well being; "Try and have a bit of a rest now before you take off again," read his motherly advice.

Before long, however, MacGowran was on his way to Spain, to appear in David Lean's film of *Doctor Zhivago*. He arrived on the set in Madrid to find his reputation had preceded him. "Oh, *you're* the actor from the Theatre of the Absurd," said Lean sarcastically.

If the tale of Yuri and Lara was bittersweet romance, the brief union of actor and director was no love story. "Under any circumstances I couldn't work happily with David Lean," said MacGowran, who played the stationmaster at Yuriatin. "He doesn't see actors as human beings, to be treated as human beings, and I can't find pleasure in working with a director of that ilk."

Early in 1965, during the run of *Waiting for Godot*, MacGowran had met a director at the opposite end of the spectrum, a young filmmaker who was enamored with Beckett. The playgoer was particularly enthralled with "this marvelous scrawny actor" playing Lucky. After a lengthy conversation — and a dozen or more cups of tea — the earnest young man decided he and Jack must work together.

MacGowran had by then established himself on the London stage as an actor who could be depended upon to deliver a performance of unusual depth and often startling power. But in his first 15 years on screen he had only two or three roles of note, few pictures like *The Quiet Man* or *Tom Jones* where he could distinguish himself. There were few directors as capable as John Ford or Tony Richardson or who crossed his path, and fewer screenwriters; there were no Becketts or O'Caseys working in film.

Jack could breathe life into the most mundane film. He had a vitality that a flat script or an inept director was rarely able to suppress, despite a lack of opportunities. In 26 features he had played an amusing assortment of small and dissatisfying parts; he brought no less energy to a role like the fanciful paleontologist in *The Giant Behemoth* than he did to *Tom Jones*, but he was ill content with the lot. Little did he realize what lay in store when he first met Roman Polanski.

The actor was considering a movie that would take him to Ireland for nine weeks when Polanski offered him a small part as a gangster in something called *Cul-de-Sac*. MacGowran had never heard of the young Polish director, who had had fame thrust upon him as the result of his first feature film, *Knife in the Water*; the money was less and they only needed him for two weeks. He was about to accept the other offer when Polanski invited him to a screening of his latest picture.

Repulsion was strong stuff — too strong for MacGowran. "If there was an accident Jack would be outside in a flash, or staring out the window; it fascinated him. But he actually had to look away from the film," recalled Gloria MacGowran. "If Polanski could do that, Jack *had* to work with him — and Roman's eagerness was a factor as well. Jack didn't think he would ever find a director he could get on with in films."

The rapport was mutual. "He was a tremendously likeable man, there's no question. I mean, there's nobody who would not like Jackie MacGowran," observed Polanski. "I had great difficulty understanding him at first; he was very amiable, but language was a barrier. Later when we went to Northumberland, to Holy Island to shoot the film, I got very close to Jack.

"First of all, working with him, I realized how exciting an actor he was. What he was doing was so funny — so right — on top of everything he was so easy to work with. On that film I had a lot of difficulties with actors. Jack emerges from this experience in my memory as the only person I could really talk to, or spend time with, besides my co-writer Gérard Brach."

Polanski and Brach had spent three years trying to sell *Cul-de-Sac*, when the success of *Repulsion* ensured financing for their bizarre black comedy. The story, which had overtones of Beckett and Pinter, centered on "three characters condemned to close proximity under isolated conditions — a study in neurosis with the thriller conventions turned upside down."

The claustrophobic environment of Holy Island provided the ideal stage for Polanski's comedy of terrors, and the worst possible working conditions. To his frustration, the already formidable challenge of putting his offbeat concepts on film was complicated by tense relation-

With Lionel Stander in Polanski's *Cul-de-Sac*, the hit of the Berlin Film Festival.

ships with his cast and cameraman, and wildly unpredictable weather. Cast and crew spent a bitterly cold summer at the remote location, at the northernmost tip of England where the sun almost never shone.

Bald, diminutive Donald Pleasence and burly Lionel Stander had been carefully chosen for the male leads and looked exactly like the characters Polanski had in mind. Françoise Dorléac had been cast in desperation at the last minute. The director found the garrulous Stander at first charming and then obnoxious; he became embroiled in arguments with Pleasence and Dorléac over things like interpretation and character motivation.

"Jack was all like butter. I'd say, 'Do this way, do that way' — he would do it," said Polanski. "With real actors, there's very little of this so- called 'motivation.'"

Stander and MacGowran played Dickie and Albie, a pair of inept gunmen on the run from a bungled crime. Albie, shot in the stomach and mortally wounded, is left alone in the car while Dickie goes to fetch help. The road, which turns out to be a causeway between the island and the mainland, is gradually covered by water. Albie nearly drowns before the car is pushed off the causeway; he dies a short time later.

Much of the dialogue proved awkward and unsuitable, owing to Polanski's lack of familiarity with the English language. But he often permitted his actors to write or improvise their own lines. "We came to a long passage, and Roman told me, 'Don't mind what's written on the paper, say anything you like.' It was a long speech which you just couldn't listen to, so I reduced it to a few words," recalled MacGowran.

Polanski treasured the spontaneity of the moment for years to come: "We were shooting the scene where Jack is in the car… and the water rises and covers the car partially. Jack is sitting in the water; he's partly conscious and almost hallucinating. He was shouting 'Richard! Richard!' And then suddenly a line escaped from his throat — 'I've got a problem!'"

MacGowran's role was brief, but physically exerting. He had never worked for a director who demanded so much of him — not even Beckett — but he admired Polanski for his dedication; he was willing to go to any length to satisfy someone who believed in perfection as much as he did. "I'd rather do 10 films for Polanski than one line for David Lean," he told a talk show host.

Polanski had never found a performer so cooperative. "When you set up the shot and lay him on the table as a corpse, in some kind of rigor mortis contortion, Jack would lay there until you said 'Stop,'" marveled the director. "Often you forget, you go to lighting, to other departments and he's laying there stiff, without moving, without budging."

MacGowran would learn that low tolerance for physical discomfort and impatience with retakes were not qualities that endeared actors to Polanski, who insisted on total submission to his direction. But he complied fully, regardless of the situation.

Jack wore a wet suit under his clothing during the causeway scene, to help insulate him from the cold. They had been filming for two hours when producer Gene Gutowski noticed the actor was turning blue; they found he was unable to talk and realized he was literally freezing to death. When they pulled him out of the car, they discovered the icy North Sea water had risen over the top of his wet suit and leaked inside.

"He absolutely never complained," said Polanski. "Jack was an actor who enjoyed the actual physical of acting — not the glory of it, not the reviews, but actually doing it, making it — an actor par excellence." The director enjoyed MacGowran's company so much he kept him on the picture the entire eight weeks they were on Holy Island.

MacGowran returned to civilization — and Beckett — in the autumn of 1965, dusting off his one-man show for the Lantern Theatre in Dublin. His decision to revive the project was met with enthusiasm, but Beckett was less happy about where it was being staged. "As you know I'm not keen on my work being done in Ireland," Sam wrote Jack. "But there's no point in bringing that up now. So I just say go ahead and good luck."

MacGowran had revised the script, with director Patrick Garland's assistance, for a presentation on BBC's *Monitor* program earlier that year. But when they took the new adaptation to Paris, Beckett's approval was not immediately forthcoming.

"Unfortunately, although he found our version correct in its content, he disapproved of its shape," recalled Garland. "There and then, in an incongruous basement bar in Saint Germain, [Beckett] set about reconstructing an entirely different one." The author came to London for rehearsals, but refused to make a personal appearance on camera.

The new Dublin production of the show, now entitled *Beginning to End*, was substantially different from *End of Day*; conspicuous by its absence was the frantic pantomime of *Act Without Words I*. The Miles Davis trumpet solo was gone too, replaced by a theme from Schubert's *Death and the Maiden*, which Becket had used in *All That Fall*.

At Beckett's suggestion, MacGowran discarded the stylized costume he had worn in 1962 and garbed himself in a large, shapeless black greatcoat. He also did away with the whiteface makeup in favor of a more realistic appearance; he now looked more like the forlorn

With Beckett and director Patrick Garland, staging *Beginning to End* for British television, 1965.

vagabond of Beckett's novels and less like a certain bowler-hatted silent film comedian.

MacGowran added a group of Beckett's poems to the program, as well as excerpts from *Embers* and the novel, *Malone Dies*. The first half of the show was now comprised of poetry and passages from the novels, the second half excerpted primarily from plays. A theme began to take shape: "the feelings and thoughts of a man faced with death."

The structure of the program still troubled Beckett, but the author hesitated to interfere. He decided that major script changes at this stage of the game would only unnerve MacGowran, whose task was difficult enough. However, he felt Lucky's monologue from *Waiting for Godot* could not possibly work out of context, and suggested that Jack replace it with something else — "whatever you fancy." But the long, rambling speech was one of the actor's favorite selections, and it remained nonetheless.

MacGowran and Beckett worked together on a spate of projects during the fall and winter of 1965-66, although getting their busy schedules to coincide was becoming increasingly difficult. Early in 1966 Jack read a selection of Beckett's poems for BBC Radio. Almost simultaneously he recorded excerpts from the one-man show, again with Sam's supervision, for a long-playing album called *MacGowran Speaking Beckett.* The author was not sure how it would work, and suggested separating the extracts by the soft stroke of a gong, letting the sound die away. Sam himself played the gong on the Claddagh Records album.

Jack recorded the material in a haunting, almost disembodied voice, per Beckett's exacting instructions. "Sam realized the monotone would not hold up theatrically but he insisted on it for the album, his work put down 'for the eyes of dogs to come.' He did the record exactly the way he wanted," noted Gloria MacGowran. "Sam always prefers it on a monotone. He doesn't like things to be, as he calls it, 'proclaimed.'"

While Beckett was in London, he directed the BBC production of *Eh Joe.* He had told the actor some time earlier that he was writing a new play for him; it did not immediately materialize, but Jack waited patiently, without even dropping a hint. On such an understanding was their relationship based.

"I haven't a gleam for the new work for you at the moment and feel sometimes that I've come to an end," Beckett had conceded a few years earlier, after abandoning *J.M. Mime.* "It's a comfort to know you understand and won't press me."

Beckett envisioned MacGowran first and foremost in his new piece designed especially for television, but he did not want the actor to feel obligated — even though the character was called "Jack" in the first draft. On sending MacGowran a revised copy of the script, he stated:

> I hope I did not seem to assume that you would necessarily want to do it because it comes from me. I assure you I don't. I do hope you will take it on. But if on reading it again and thinking it over you decide it's not for you, no one would better understand than I.
> —Letter to MacGowran, May 15, 1965

Of the three finished projects Beckett wrote with MacGowran in mind, none would provide a greater challenge than *Eh Joe.* Like Krapp, and Henry of *Embers,* Joe was a man tormented by his past. The play — Beckett's first for television — was similar to *Krapp's Last Tape* in content and form; it was a dramatization of self-perception not unlike *Film,* but refined in technique.

The script depicted a man alone in a room — a persistent Beckett

Tormented by a voice in his head in *Eh Joe*, written for MacGowran — and directed — by Beckett.

motif. MacGowran was called upon to shuffle from bed to window to door to cupboard to bed, making certain he was not being watched. He then sat on the edge of the bed and began to relax, only to be assaulted by a voice inside his skull. The camera moved in ever closer on his guilt-ridden face, as the almost colorless, knife-edged female voice from "that penny farthing hell you call your mind" accused and taunted him mercilessly.

Eh Joe was, in essence, one step further into the abyss:

> Joe is Mr. Beckett's man in the only situation Mr. Beckett has bothered to consider since *Waiting for Godot*: everything is over and nothing has been worth the effort it has cost...
> — *The Times*, July 5, 1966

As with *Endgame*, Beckett again refused to take credit for directing the production. Few directors could have abided the author's staging instructions, which called for the camera to make "nine slight moves in towards face, say four inches each time," between the first and last potent close-up of MacGowran's striking countenance. "Face: Practically motionless throughout, eyes unblinking... impassive except in so far as it reflects the mounting tension of *listening*," dictated the script.

No sooner had MacGowran finished *Eh Joe* when his services were again requested by Roman Polanski, the only associate of Jack's whose zeal for perfection ever approached that of Beckett. This time Roman had Jack in mind for the leading role in a zany departure from his psychological horror films.

During a social evening, producer Gene Gutowski had told Polanski an old music hall joke about a Jewish vampire being confronted by a crucifix: "Oy, have you got the wrong vampire." Polanski laughed, and the inspiration for *The Vampire Killers* was born. He and collaborator Gérard Brach began to build around the gag, concocting a recipe that called for large quantities of blood and garlic, fangs and wooden stakes, and a nutty professor who had stepped straight out of a cartoon.

"I had a very hard time on *Cul-de-Sac* but I had a fantastic experience with Jack and the next script I decided to write for him," recalled Polanski. "I just wanted to make a film with him; the role of the professor was written for him from the beginning to the end.

"While we were on Holy Island, I was often making caricatures of Jack and we were all laughing about him, his nose, his eyes, et cetera. I later started adding a moustache to it, and long hair, eventually a top hat and we came up with this character. I wanted to make a comedy, a sort of fairy tale — and that's how I saw him. I wanted him to have this

As Professor Abronsius in Polanski's *Dance of the Vampires*, which found a cult following in the U.S. as *The Fearless Vampire Killers*.

Roman Polanski in a dual role: actor and director.

slightly Einstein-like look, and I knew Jack would fit it. I mean, he was a genius in this part."

The eccentric scientist, as conceived by Polanski, was a role that called for a very physical, athletic kind of performance. It was a dream part, the lead buffoon in a knockabout comedy of the sort that was earmarked for extinction with the arrival of talking pictures.

As Buster Keaton had come to realize in the twenties — and Jacques Tati was to rediscover in the forties — the constituent of silent comedy was the long shot. The face mattered not nearly so much as the physique; what an actor did with his body and how he carried it about with him were all important. The rubbery walk, the suspicious posture and the genteel waltz of Professor Abronsius, as executed by MacGowran, were the graceful touches of an actor who had cultivated the coordination of mind and body to a high art.

Dance of the Vampires, as the picture was eventually titled, was in a sense one long, flawlessly choreographed sight gag. In the course of the film the script called for MacGowran to become frozen solid, get clobbered by a salami and drenched with wine, mimic a bat in flight, do the minuet and scratch his back against a bedpost like a cat. Most of his antics were filmed in London on the backlot of MGM's Borehamwood studio, due to a mysterious "warm spell" in the Italian alps that melted all the snow.

In one long, memorable sequence, Abronsius and his youthful assistant, Alfred — played by Polanski himself — climb out a castle window with a case of wooden stakes in hand, crawl along the cornice, and jump onto the roof of a crypt. After falling onto and sliding down an even narrower rooftop, they try to gain entrance through a window vent. Alfred enters easily, feet first; the professor makes the mistake of going in head first, with dire results, as indicated in the script:

> ABRONSIUS is in a nasty situation. He has made such a bungle of things that he is jammed with his arms stuck alongside his body. He hasn't managed to get through the vent any further than the elbows. Only the head and shoulders appear as though of a gargoyle. His muffler and glasses dangle absurdly.

Alfred seizes the professor's head and tugs. Abronsius doesn't budge. The assistant nearly strangles the professor, then pulls on Abronsius' muffler, to no avail. After proving incompetent in fulfilling their sacred mission — to destroy the vampires by driving stakes into their hearts — Alfred disappears into the castle. Later, he glances out a window to see two legs — the professor's — still sticking out of the vent. They are frozen stiff. Alfred goes out on the roof, puts the case of stakes down, and tries to move the legs:

> ALFRED starts to tug fiercely in order to dislodge ABRONSIUS from the vent. He takes a great risk for his foothold is narrow and slippery and he has his back to open space.
>
> Suddenly the PROFESSOR wrenches himself free from the grip of the stone; ALFRED surprised and losing his balance just stops short of the edge of the abyss, with the Professor glued tightly to him. He waves his arms and with a desperate jerk of the hips manages to avoid falling off.
>
> ABRONSIUS is purple; his eyes brimming with frozen tears start out of their sockets. The light blinds him. He moves his foot and knocks the case, which starts to slide towards the edge of the roof. ALFRED, who is supporting his master stiff as a post, lets go of him, wishing to catch the case before it disappears, but ABRONSIUS falls on top of him. He grasps him, letting the precious case slide away.

"I can see now, when I look back, that a lot of funny things in the script were inspired by Jack's behavior and by funny things about him," said Polanski. His patience, lying on the table stiff [during the filming of *Cul-de-Sac*] until someone notices he's no more needed — inspired things like him being stuck in that window forever, with his nose dripping ice."

Dance of the Vampires, which co-starred Roman's then-girlfriend, Sharon Tate, proved hugely popular at the box office in almost every country it played. The sole exceptions were the United States and Canada, where it was released in a "butchered" version as *The Fearless Vampire Killers, or Pardon Me, But Your Teeth Are in My Neck*. That executive producer Martin Ransohoff cut the film for American audiences — and re-dubbed his and MacGowran's voices — rankled Polanski for years.

"He ruined it completely — it is not the same picture," lamented the director, who was forced to withdraw it from the Berlin Film Festival and attempted to remove his name from the credits. Polanski's original cut became a cult film in European cinemas; an "uncut version," restoring the actor's voices and some — but not all — of the missing footage, eventually turned up in U.S. revival cinemas.

9

If Roman Polanski never ceased to be amazed at MacGowran's acting abilities, he was even more astonished at Jack's energy and stamina. "He could take tremendous endurance," marveled Polanski. "You could not exhaust that man."

MacGowran labored long and hard on *Dance of the Vampires*, from late February of 1966 through late July. Shooting was scheduled for 10 weeks and took 20 to complete. Even when they had wrapped the last scene, neither he nor Polanski could let go; Roman delighted in carrying Jack around on his back at parties, recreating a cherished moment from the picture.

During the final weeks of filming, MacGowran found himself the servant of two masters. He worked from dawn to dusk at the studios, then rushed home and quickly ate his supper, or went without if he was running late. In the evening, he rehearsed his role as Joxer Daly for a forthcoming Dublin revival of *Juno and the Paycock*.

Despite his familiarity with the play, MacGowran had never done a professional stage production — save the ill-conceived New York *Juno* — and he relished the opportunity; he had turned down Laurence Olivier's invitation to join the recent National Theatre revival, due to a scheduling conflict.

While he was on first call to Polanski, he gave himself as completely to one task as he did the other. "Jack was giving a full performance at the first reading of the play. He built on it from there," said producer Fred O'Donovan. "Most actors don't end up at the level he started on. But MacGowran never 'acted' — he lived the part."

When O'Donovan asked the actor who would make a good Captain Boyle, Jack recommended Peter O'Toole. It was an auspicious choice — and a disastrous idea. The fact that MacGowran had the *starring* role in the Polanski film drove O'Toole berserk, especially since he was unemployed; Peter insisted they begin work immediately on the O'Casey play, even though the film was not yet completed.

Rehearsals commenced smoothly in London, but as the stew began to simmer, artistic temperaments flared up and volatile egos boiled over. MacGowran's longtime friendship with O'Toole quickly disintegrated, its deterioration marked by violent rows, mistrust, disloyalty and spite.

Siobhán McKenna, who played Juno Boyle, recalled the night of "the incident": "One evening I was told I wasn't needed for rehearsal. They were only doing Captain-Joxer scenes, but Juno is in a lot of them so I went down anyway," she said. "As I arrived, [director] Denis Carey and [co-producer] Jules Buck had Jackie pinned against the wall. 'You do one or you do the other — the play or the film,' they told him."

The following evening called for a full rehearsal. MacGowran had already put in a 12-hour day before he got there. He was lackluster but steady through the end of the second act; he was exhausted by then, but felt he had to do the third. Part way through he collapsed and they rushed him to the hospital.

"I don't think the rows and things would have had the effect they did, but Jack was so wrapped up in Professor Abronsius," said Gloria MacGowran. "He *was* the professor. He was the professor all day, and then at night he'd go out and he *was* Joxer. Jack cracked under outside influences, never the play or the film. He thrived on work."

That MacGowran almost suffered a nervous breakdown was no surprise to those around him. Many of them advised him to withdraw from the play when they saw the batteries running down, but he refused to listen. "I can do it, old scout," he assured O'Toole. MacGowran couldn't bear to let anyone down; he was determined to live up to and beyond other people's expectations of him, even at the expense of his health.

"Polanski and I were both demanding the best from him. It took its toll," affirmed Fred O'Donovan. "Jack was a fragile man, a quiet, gentle soul, but there must've been great turmoil inside. He could never say 'no' to anyone; it created enormous problems for him."

MacGowran had always played in support of O'Toole, but with their roles nearly equal Peter found himself at a disadvantage. Jack was no longer the drinking partner he could make a fool of, as he had in Stratford; MacGowran sober had a stage presence the popular film star couldn't begin to compete with.

O'Toole met with harsh criticism when he failed to master the O'Casey vocal rhythm and Dublin idiom. Despite the actor's frequent claims of having been born in Ireland, his brogue was inexplicably laced with traces of Cockney, as well as his native Liverpool dialect.

With his back turned to the audience in one scene, Peter could hear people laughing, but he couldn't know what they were laughing at. He accused Jack of doing "cheap stuff" to upstage him. "I don't give a fuck if you come in naked on a bicycle," he yelled backstage. "Just let me know."

O'Toole had ordered a pair of bushy eyebrows from a London wig

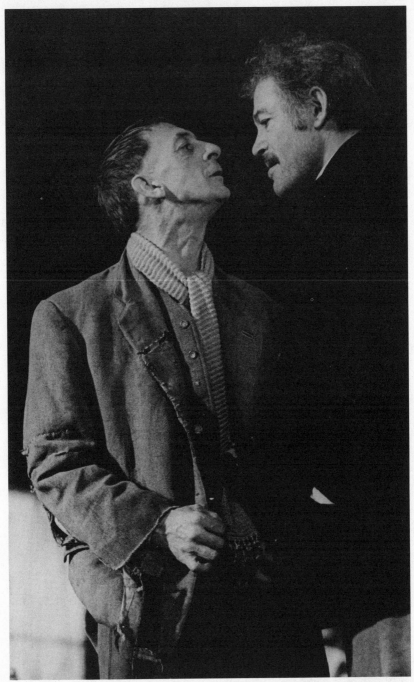

Photo by Michael O'Reilly

Battling buddies: Jack MacGowran and Peter O'Toole were at odds on and off stage, during the Gaiety Theatre production of *Juno and the Paycock*. Dublin, 1966.

salon. The night they arrived, Captain Boyle dropped them into a frying pan in place of the usual pork sausages. "Eat your eyebrows," he ordered Joxer. By the end of the two week run at the Gaiety Theatre, Peter was relying on the gimmicks he had accused Jack of earlier.

MacGowran was clearly a threat; he was a hometown boy and the audiences adored him. He had polished the characterization at every opportunity until it was flawless, avoiding all the by-now-familiar pitfalls. His portrayal was far from the Abbey stereotype of the garrulous, shoulder-shrugging imp. It was the *real* Joxer — a slimy, sniveling leech, straight from the Dublin sewers, as Jack had always wanted to play him.

> This Joxer is a cross between a Shakespearean Fool and a gutter rat, packed with jerkily visual comedy, but basically full of a sort of rodent malignance that bares its teeth when the people it sponges on meet disaster. It's a terrifyingly powerful performance; one that will be remembered with respect — and a lot of unease.
> — Séamus Kelly, *The Irish Times*,
> August 3, 1966

"Jack stole the show completely. In many ways he was a better Joxer than F.J. McCormick," asserted Séamus Kelly, elaborating on his review. "McCormick made Joxer an easy-going gutter snipe, whereas Jack was that on the surface — but when he was crossed, he showed the rat's teeth."

By all accounts, MacGowran deserved — and should have taken — a much- needed rest when his stint in the O'Casey play was over. Instead he joined the cast of Richard Lester's surrealistic film comedy, *How I Won the War*. Michael Crawford and John Lennon got top billing, but Jack inadvertently stole the spotlight, as he had at the Gaiety.

The actors saw only fragments of the script as they ad-libbed their way through most of the picture. MacGowran outfitted himself as a minstrel man, impersonated a general and basically ran amok in the role of Private Juniper. As the film progressed, his characterization outgrew the others.

While wholesale improvisation was encouraged, producer-director Lester had more in mind than entertainment. He wanted to make an anti-war film that would not encourage war, glamorize it or treat it nostalgically, as he felt previous "anti-war" films had done. He chose World War II as his backdrop over Vietnam, because "taking an absurd war and showing it as absurd is too easy."

Lester also decided to make use of "the theatre of the absurd and

With Ronald Lacey and John Lennon, on the set of *How I Won the War*.

the theatre of alienation" as part of his battleplan, hoping to strike a balance "between slapstick of the absurd and horror of the absurd." While one film critic would decide that MacGowran's clown-soldier "could have stepped from the plays of Beckett," the works of Ionesco appeared to be a more predominant influence.

But MacGowran spread the gospel, as it were, while on location in Almeria, Spain. "Jack turned me onto Beckett while we were down there," John Lennon later recalled. "He gave me his copy of *Krapp's Last Tape*. It was just about a guy talking into a tape recorder. I flipped over it — that's all I've done since I was 13 years old."

Beckett was, in any case, a welcome diversion between scenes. "It was a madhouse down there; there was nothing to do but party. It was like some weird psycho drama," said Lennon, who was then on leave from the Beatles. "We didn't know what to make of the film; it had something to do with war. I asked Dick Lester what he wanted. He said, 'Power.' Jack kept us all going with his mad bits, but the film never got free-flowing."

By the time he had shot his last scene, MacGowran found himself suffering from a severe case of fatigue and nervous exhaustion, and checked into a London hospital to recuperate. He rarely paid any attention to his health — he loathed doctors and hospitals — but he was physically and emotionally spent.

MacGowran had never been fully rehabilitated after his near-fatal bout with alcoholism. Neither he nor Gloria realized the extent of the disease, or the fundamental damage it had done, until it was too late. They didn't know that abstinence was only a small part of the prescription, that proper therapy treated the whole man.

Jack's negative emotional posture and spiritual deterioration were never tended to, nor were his physical problems. He failed to come to grips with the inner conflicts that compelled him to drink and created his negative attitudes; failure to recognize them only increased the pain.

"He had a good torment going for him, and maybe his was a little more than most. Anybody who has to give up drink to the extent that Jackie did, never quite gets over the problem spiritually," said his friend, Burgess Meredith. "He never seemed to be quite free from the shadows. He wasn't saying, 'I feel like a drink,' or anything like that, but it made its mark.

"I never saw him impose any problems on anyone, ever. People would sense that he was vulnerable and rather helpless. I don't know anybody else who had that capacity where you felt responsible, and liked to be responsible, for their well being. But I felt that way about

Jackie and I think most people did — certainly Beckett."

Sam Beckett was closely attuned to MacGowran's needs. He was as keenly aware of Jack's mental and physical state as the ebb and flow of his own creative juices. Sam knew how Jack felt without a word being uttered. He would sense the actor was in financial trouble, and ease the burden in any way he could, without being asked.

Early in 1967, before he had fully recovered from his breakdown, MacGowran agreed to do Beckett's *Imagination Dead Imagine* for BBC Radio. Jack was almost always Sam's first choice whenever the BBC produced any of his work. MacGowran had neither the will nor the inclination to turn Beckett down; the fact that he was not up to it physically did not restrain him from accepting the job.

But he could make things hectic for those who had to work around him. "Jack was very difficult to pin down, he was so neurotic," said drama critic Martin Esslin, then head of BBC Radio Drama. "I would book a studio — which has to be done weeks in advance — and Gloria would ring that day and say, 'Jack's not well, he can't do it.' I think *Imagination Dead Imagine* was postponed three times.

"Jack was lucky he was so unique. If it had been anybody else, the BBC would have said, 'Don't use him.' But Jack was so special; when it came to doing Beckett, he was indispensable. Sam adored Jack. He was conscious of the fact that Jack did almost by telepathy exactly what Sam wanted him to do."

MacGowran was nearly as indispensable to O'Casey as he was to Beckett, in the minds of many producers. He was still not well — and still unable to say no — when he was invited to reprise his role as Seamus Shields in *The Shadow of a Gunman* at the Mermaid Theatre that spring. Jack further increased the burden on himself by directing the production, and playing two shows a night.

Humble beginnings ever in mind, MacGowran was particularly sympathetic to anyone trying to get a start. He fleshed out the cast with actors who had not yet had a chance to prove themselves; Shivaun O'Casey, the playwright's daughter, played the female lead. But Jack's choices did not always make for good ensemble acting.

During the run, MacGowran announced plans to present one or two plays a year at the Mermaid, and direct O'Casey's *Cock-a-Doodle-Dandy* there. He also announced his desire to direct a new production of *Waiting for Godot*. But his warmly received return to the London stage in *Shadow* was to mark his final appearance there, as actor or director.

Jack was not the only one who wanted to direct *Godot* that year. Roman Polanski also wanted to do it — as a film. He and Jack had talked continually about Beckett's work on the set of their two collaborations, and about the possibilities of putting the play on screen. They also went to Paris to talk to Beckett — with predictable results.

"We had several conversations about it at different times, but he always insisted it was not a good piece for film," said Polanski. "Maybe he didn't believe it could be done. But I did, and I wanted to do it very faithfully."

However, Beckett was adamant in his decision:

> I'm terribly sorry to disappoint you and Polanski but I don't want any film of *Godot*. As it stands it is simply not cinema material. And adaptation would destroy it. Please forgive me ...and don't think of me as a purist bastard.
>
> —Letter to MacGowran, December 13, 1967

MacGowran was busy playing the starring role in a film dreamed up by Polanski's writing partner, Gérard Brach, when the rejection came from Beckett. *Wonderwall* was fun, and full of wild sight gags, but it was long way from *Waiting for Godot* or even *Dance of the Vampires*. Jack loved the script — which cast him as an absent-minded entomologist — but could only pretend he was happy with director Joe Massot.

He emerged from the project to find film offers pouring in. With the release of Polanski's vampire spoof and the BBC sale of *Beginning to End* to European television, the opportunities — and the demands on his fragile health — began to multiply exponentially.

James Mason made a special trip to Paris to see *Dance of the Vampires* when it opened. He had seen Jack's one-man show in Dublin, and had been raving ever since, to anyone who would listen; now he wanted MacGowran as his co-star for a film to be made in Australia. Columbia Pictures was intent on casting an American actor as Mason's ne'er-do-well buddy in *Age of Consent*. But once Mason had seen MacGowran cavorting as Professor Abronsius, he insisted; when the studio refused to yield, he flew Jack to North Queensland at his own expense, three weeks ahead of the unit.

Mason was rewarded for his obstinacy by a kinetic performance. "If I were to recommend *Age of Consent* to anyone, I would do so 80% on the strength of Jackie's presence in it," said Mason, who co-produced the picture. "He identified completely with the shoddy little character he was playing — a rough Australian bludger — and he played it with total credibility and enormous fun."

While on location on the Great Barrier Reef, MacGowran received a number of invitations to lecture on Beckett. At his first opportunity he

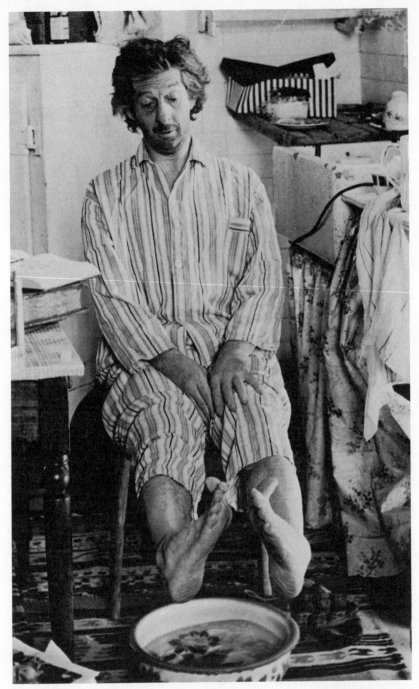

As Professor Collins in the zany *Wonderwall*.

performed excerpts from *Beginning to End* at Macquarie University and engaged in a discussion with the students; he was asked to return to Sydney with the complete show the following year, but other commitments prevented his acceptance.

A plan to do the Beckett anthology in London did not materialize, but MacGowran took it up to Ulster for the Belfast 68 festival. In the United States, Burgess Meredith and Omar Sharif worked out a plan to present their mutual friend in his one-man show on a tour of universities, but again the idea fell through. Beckett, meanwhile, was thinking about writing a new television play for Jack — "perhaps the old idea of the man waiting in a room" — but nothing came of that either.

MacGowran did not want for employment in 1968, however. Shortly after he returned from Australia, he was off to Europe for a farce about the French Revolution. *Start the Revolution Without Me* — which featured longtime friend and fellow Beckett interpreter Billie Whitelaw — gave Jack an unusually zany role as the leader of the peasant army. He spent weeks filming in a damp muddy cave 40 miles outside Paris, only to have many of his scenes cut out — but there were other compensations.

"This was one of the rare opportunities for Jack not to have to do a precise piece of work. I think he found it refreshing to work as wide open and loose as we did on this thing; it wasn't written by an important writer like Beckett, where we had to be faithful to every word," said director Bud Yorkin, who was immeasurably fond of the actor.

"He had that wonderful, wonderful face and body and voice. You could never replace or find another Jack MacGowran if you looked for that kind of performer, a man who could go from the insanity of *Tom Jones* or *Start the Revolution* to Shakespeare or Beckett."

Not all of Jack's associates had such high regard for his talents. Throughout his career, the various agents, managers and theatrical producers he affiliated with were prone to take advantage of him. His agents, in particular, were a succession of unscrupulous individuals who generally acted in their own best interests.

Only during the last five years of his career was he represented by people who genuinely cared about him, like Maggie Parker and Robert Lantz. "Jackie was very vulnerable — he only lived when he acted. He unfortunately had to depend on a lot of people not as erudite as himself," said Parker, who handled MacGowran in London during the late sixties. "I cherished him."

Parker was all ears when producer Michael Birkett mentioned matter-of-factly that he and Peter Brook had been unable to find

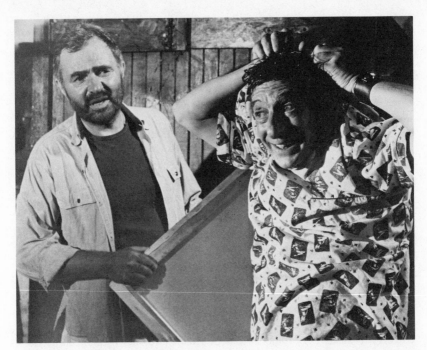

With James Mason in *Age of Consent*.

Courtesy of Gloria MacGowran

With Billie Whitelaw, between takes on *Start the Revolution Without Me*.

anyone to play the Fool in their upcoming film of *King Lear*. She advised Lord Birkett that her client, James Mason, had long desired to play Lear with MacGowran as his Fool.

Paul Scofield had given a powerful performance in the title role seven years earlier, under Brook's direction, and was already set to reprise his stage portrayal. The choice of Beckett's foremost interpreter as the Fool was less predictable, but almost inevitable.

In adapting *Lear* for contemporary audiences, Peter Brook took inspiration in Jan Kott's essay, *"King Lear* or *Endgame"* — in which the Polish critic found in Beckett a grotesquerie that was a mutant of Greek and Elizabethan tragedy; and in the mouth of Shakespeare's motley-clad sage, the surreal language of the modern theatre. The production was not based on Kott's analysis, but there was a great identity of views.

Brook's film version — photographed in the frozen wasteland of Skaagen, Denmark, that was more than a little suggestive of Beckett country — was every bit as bold and uncompromising as his landmark stage production. Excising exposition and subplot, continuity and spectacle, the director experimented relentlessly. He tried to evolve "an impressionistic movie technique," hoping his visual and aural assault on the viewer could capture "Shakespeare's rough, uneven, jagged and disconcerting vision."

Though the interaction between Lear and his Fool was pared to the bone — as was everything else in the play — the intimacy of their relationship was one of the strengths of the film. There was a mutual respect off screen as well. "The first time I saw Jack, in *Endgame* at the Aldwych Theatre, I came away haunted by the impression he made on me," remembered Paul Scofield. "Nijinsky said in his diary he knew how to *surprise* an audience. So did Jack."

MacGowran also surprised his director. When the script called for Jack to sing a song — for a scene where Lear and the Fool take the coach to Gloucester's castle — Brook asked him to suggest something he knew. Jack said he'd prefer to improvise; when he was asked to do the song the following day, he refused. "When the cameras roll, I'll sing," he insisted. Brook was taken aback; he was not used to being addressed in such a manner. When they shot the scene, Jack ad-libbed the song — to the director's unstinting approval.

Filming *King Lear* was an ordeal for MacGowran. The physical demands of filming in sub-zero weather were almost too much for him at times. Nor was Shakespeare one of his favorite writers; he had played most of the jesters at some point in his career, to little satisfac-

As the Fool in *King Lear*, teasing Paul Scofield with "the two crowns of the egg."

tion. But once he discussed the film with Brook, and understood what he was doing, he enjoyed himself in the role.

Ultimately, MacGowran played the part as though he had been born to it. "All his earlier work was present in the Fool," said Cyril Cusack, who portrayed the Duke of Albany. "What Jack brought from his background was a reality to the performance. It was not theatrical at all; it was real, as Shakespeare must have intended it."

That he was known primarily for his comedic ability was a source of irritation to MacGowran. He was upset by the lack of serious dramatic material like *Lear* that was offered him. But he had an innate comic sense; he knew instinctively when something was funny and when it was not, to the nuances that often escaped others.

As he grew older, MacGowran became dead serious about his work. Weighed down by his worldly burdens, he channeled his energies into the characters he played. He was far more comfortable in their skin than his own, and his gave to his dramatis personae his vitality, his strength and effervescence.

"If he found something funny himself, it was no longer funny," said Gloria MacGowran. "If a director laughed at something he did, some little facet of a character, it really angered him. Jack felt they were there to judge whether a thing was funny or not, not to laugh at it. Beckett and Polanski he didn't mind — they did it in a different way. Roman would walk over and hug him if he did something particularly beautiful.

"Jack used to say, in making others laugh, you lose the ability to laugh yourself. He firmly believed it; he laughed less and less as time went on."

10

MacGowran spent the winter of 1968-69 filming *King Lear* in North Jutland, with Gloria and his young daughter Tara keeping him company on location. He was thawed by the warmth of old friends when Burgess Meredith welcomed him home, by sending Jack the script for a film project that would reunite them together with James Mason.

That fall the triumvirate traveled to Hong Kong to make *The Yin and the Yang of Mr. Go*, starring Mason as an unscrupulous power broker and MacGowran as a dedicated CIA agent — with Meredith directing his own screenplay. The film was halted in mid-production for lack of funds and never completed.

Mason had suspected there was a problem at the outset, but assumed producer Thomas Ian Ross could raise further capital when the money ran out; he felt sure the backers would come through, if only to protect their initial investment. When Ross disappeared and left them stranded, Mason gamely carried on. Many of his friends were involved in the picture and he was particularly anxious to see some money fall into MacGowran's hands.

"Jackie never got paid his full salary and neither did any of us," lamented Meredith. "One time we couldn't finish a scene — there was no money available — and poor Jackie had just gotten his first paycheck. I borrowed the money back from him to pay these Chinese extras, these big strong stuntmen we were afraid would murder us if we didn't pay them."

Without the participation or permission of the principals, the extant footage was later assembled with an offscreen narrative to bridge the gaps; it eventually "escaped" long enough to be test-marketed, but was never released. "What 'escaped' must have been awful," said Meredith. "Many key scenes were never shot. We could never get the film together to finish it, though we would have liked to — but Ross had sold so many parts of the film so many times, and we couldn't even find him."

A more responsible associate of MacGowran's also disappeared in the fall of 1969, at least temporarily. Samuel Beckett was hiding out in a small village in Tunisia that October, when the announcement came that he had won the Nobel Prize for Literature. The newsmen who intruded on his privacy were permitted only to photograph his cragged countenance; once again he refused to make statements or answer questions.

The 63-year-old Beckett, who was recovering from a lung abscess, was less than ecstatic about the honor. He felt he was not entitled to the prize because James Joyce had been denied it, and he disdained the notoriety that came with it. The reaction of *L'Exprês* was typical: "Giving the Nobel Prize to Beckett is tantamount to crowning literature itself."

But the award was in short "the last thing Mr. Beckett wanted," said his French publisher, Jérôme Lindon. Failing to dissuade the Swedish Academy from naming him the Nobel laureate, Beckett sent Lindon to Stockholm to accept the prize on his behalf. Academy secretary Karl Ragnar Gierow acknowledged Beckett's pessimism but observed:

> [his work is] cleansed by a love of mankind that grows in understanding as it plumbs further into the depths of abhorrence... from that position, in the realms of annihilation, the writing of Samuel Beckett rises like a miserere from all mankind, its muffled minor key sounding liberation to the oppressed and comfort to those in need.

Coinciding with the announcement of Beckett's selection, *The Times* reported that MacGowran would present "a new solo entertainment" drawn from the laureate's work, in Paris the following January. The show, which Jack and Sam had discussed before the actor went to Hong Kong, was subsequently slated for New York, London and West Germany.

Beckett set forth the conditions under which he and MacGowran would again collaborate. Jack's agent would have to make arrangements with Grove Press, which controlled the performing rights to Beckett's work in the U.S. But the author insisted, "I don't want any royalties from this production and would like them to go to you. So tell your agent to proceed on that basis."

Filmmaking was a challenging if not always pleasant or prosperous diversion, and the requisite travel satisfied the wanderlust in MacGowran. But his devotion to the theatre, and to Beckett, was unrelenting. Sam Beckett's words were the boundaries of his world, like the protagonist of *Watt*, "from the door to the window, from the window to the bed; from the bed to the window, from the window to the door." There was no exit — they were two men sharing the same soul.

Both were Dublin born and Dublin bred, and both had fled their homeland when it threatened to suffocate them artistically. But Ireland had never left them, as it had never left Joyce or O'Casey. "Jack was one of the few if not the only Irishman who broke out of 'Irishry' without losing his root, his Irish strength," said Peter O'Toole. "He was the only actor in my generation who fought it and won."

Sam's reputation had grown immeasurably in the 12 years Jack had known him. Though he resented the encroaching limelight as much as ever, the author was less shy and withdrawn; while he made no concessions to his public, he had mellowed with age. And if he still felt his every word was "like an unnecessary stain on silence and nothingness," a new generation thought he had something to say.

But where people had once seen only gloom and doom, MacGowran felt perhaps they were ready to discover the life-affirming qualities inherent in Beckett's work — the savage wit, the proud defiance, the innate dignity and moreover, the courage — the ability to laugh at the human predicament even as man teetered at the brink of annihilation.

Beckett, above all, did not embrace "the lust for despair" — as O'Casey had once maligned him. "No matter how you approach Beckett, through his novels or his plays, no matter what setting he places his characters in for dramatic purposes, never will they give way to despair," observed MacGowran. "The key word in all his plays is 'perhaps'... and therein lies the hope that there's a fifty-fifty chance of things going our way."

Nor did MacGowran view Beckett as "the high priest of the absurd," as the author was so widely perceived. Unlike Ionesco, Beckett had a serious vision of life. He was an absurdist only in the sense Camus once defined: "a life lived solely for its own sake in a universe that no longer made sense because there was no God to resolve the contradictions."

MacGowran and Beckett had yet to resolve the problems of *Beginning to End* to their satisfaction. Sam had never been entirely happy with Jack's concept of the one-man show, neither in its first manifestation as *End of Day* in 1962, nor in subsequent editions. Although he had helped reconstruct the show when Jack adapted it for the BBC in 1965, and gave his blessing for the Lantern Theatre production in Dublin that year, there was something awry. Though MacGowran had sought — and received — Beckett's cooperation through all its incarnations, the anthology was still a work-in-progress not wholly satisfactory.

The challenge was clear as Beckett and MacGowran met in Paris to discuss the show. The problem was not so much one of selection as one of form. *Beginning to End* lacked connective tissue; it wanted for emotional logic and continuity, a common thread to hold the audience between one segment and the next.

Jack and Sam decided to start from scratch, reshaping the program with rapt attention to structure and content. No longer would it be a potpourri, a hodgepodge of delectable tidbits snipped impulsively from the author's work, but a homage to Beckett's *œuvre*: "the story of a man's innermost thoughts on the statement that he's going to die," observed MacGowran, "and along the way... the man's past, his hopes, his relationships to parents and people, the attitudes and the terror he feels as the end approaches."

In assimilating the novels, plays and poems, MacGowran had come to the realization that Beckett's "people" were all of the same mind and marrow, the same steady, unmistakable voice. Molloy, communicating with his aged mother by knocking on her skull — "that she should associate the four knocks with anything but money was something to be avoided at all costs" — and pondering the insoluble problem of the sucking stones... Malone, speculating on the number of his days... The Unnamable, finding the courage to go on...

Watt, blathering about his genealogy — "my earth and my father's and my mother's and my father's father's and my mother's mother's and my father's mother's and my mother's father's" — or rhapsodizing on the change of seasons... Krapp, dredging up the bones of an old love... Lucky, spewing his mad soliloquy... Clov, departing, embers glowing to light the way... one and the same, black-humored clowns parading down the strand. Cloaked in a weathered greatcoat from heel to throat, they wandered to and fro, turn and turn about, from beginning to end.

From their outward appearance to their inner rhythms, MacGowran was a keen observer and mimic of others. He had developed a talent for observation as a small boy, taking the train from Dublin to nearby Dalkey and back just to people watch; he studied men, women and children, absorbing everyone's way of walking, looking and talking. To Jack's trained eye there was a Catholic walk and a Protestant walk, a distinction he drew for the amusement of family and friends.

He studied pigeons and chickens intently, emulating the twitch and thrust of the neck and the snap-back of the head. He borrowed mannerisms from cartoon characters — Sylvester, the bird-chasing cat, fascinated him no end — and mimicked his pals and neighbors. Their smallest idiosyncrasies did not escape his attention.

If he called upon his every resource in creating the tattered vagabond of *Beginning to End*, MacGowran did not have to journey far for

Discussing the one-man show with Samuel Beckett, and rehearsing, below, with director Patrick Garland. London, 1965.

inspiration. The character was no stranger, for Beckett had drawn him from the streets of Dublin they both knew all too well.

The Beckett Man who took the stage was a composite of all the deliciously eccentric old down-and-outs who wandered the streets of their hometown, in the very same ankle-length greatcoat. MacGowran had watched them fishing from the River Liffey with a bicycle wheel, a length of string and a hook; he had followed them in and out of "spit and sawdust" pubs, down O'Connell Street, along the Quays and through the alley ways as they mumbled to themselves, launched into incomprehensible tirades and danced to the beat of drums only they could hear. On one occasion, Jack found a derelict who had no place to sleep, and took him home for the night like a stray dog.

The character who represented Beckett's indefatigable heroes developed gradually. The disembodied voice Jack had employed for *MacGowran Speaking Beckett* was relinquished, along with the pathetic deadpan expression he had worn throughout the first *Beginning to End*; he had smiled then but once, the corners of his mouth curling momentarily into an impish grin — to devastating effect.

Housed in MacGowran's elastic body and electric voice, his liquid movements and shocking expressions, the little fellow finally came to life in Paris. He laughed. He wept. He snarled. He pouted. He brooded; he raged. He scratched his behind. He stood, he sat, he hobbled. And he danced.

But the actor made sparing use of gestures, reducing everything to a bare minimum; his hands he kept in his pockets, or at his sides, for much of the time. His every move dictated by the script, MacGowran used instead the shift of his head and the turn of his neck, the slant of his bearing and the manner of his gait.

Simplicity was of the essence. Miles Davis and Franz Schubert were discarded, along with the music of the seashore manufactured by the BBC's Radiophonic Workshop; the sea filtered naturally through *Embers* but was superfluous here. MacGowran also divested himself of the accoutrements he had used in previous versions of the show, the bowler hat, knapsack and walking stick.

"In the early stage of Jack's involvement with Beckett, there was absolute confusion," asserted Peter O'Toole. "When he began to digest Beckett further, it was like a clear spring — a flow of complicated material delivered in an uncomplicated way. He began to comprehend with his toes."

As his understanding of Sam's work grew, Jack's performance became insanely comical. More and more, he realized, the misfits who peopled the Beckett landscape were blood brothers to the silent film

Beginning to End on Irish TV, 1966.

comics and music hall clowns both actor and author had so admired in their youth.

When Jack asked Sam how much laughter he expected from the show, the answer came readily: "As much as you can get." The stuff of Beckett was tragi*comedy*, not morbidity and despair. Somehow, it had gotten turned around. "People find Beckett morose," MacGowran said once in disbelief. "I find him *so* funny."

Few passages in modern literature, he felt sure, could be funnier than the sequence in which Molloy calculates with impeccable logic the circulation of 16 pebbles, or sucking stones, transferring them among his pockets one by one, then four by four, and finally devises a mathematical progression of "sucks and transfers" in order to guarantee "not one sucked twice, not one left unsucked."

> All (all!) that was necessary was to put for example, to begin with, six stones in the right pocket of my greatcoat, or supply-pocket, five in the right pocket of my trousers, and five in the left pocket of my trousers, that makes the lot, twice five ten plus six sixteen, and none, for none remained, in the left pocket of my greatcoat, which for the time being remained empty...Good. Now I can begin to suck. Watch me closely. I take a stone from the right pocket of my greatcoat, the one empty. I take a second stone from the right pocket of my greatcoat, suck it, put it in the left pocket of my greatcoat. And so on until the right pocket of my greatcoat is empty and the six stones I have just sucked...are all in the left pocket of my greatcoat. Pausing then, and concentrating, so as not to make a balls of it, I transfer to the right pocket of my greatcoat, in which there are no stones left, the five stones in the right pocket of my trousers, which I replace by the five stones in the left pocket of my trousers, which I replace by the six stones in the left pocket of my greatcoat...

> But deep down I didn't give a tinker's curse...it was all the same to me whether I sucked a different stone each time or always the same stone, until the end of time. For they all tasted exactly the same. And if I had collected sixteen, it was not...to suck them turn and turn about, but simply to have a little store, so as never to be without. But deep down I didn't give a fiddler's damn about being without, when they were all gone they would be all gone, I wouldn't be the worse off, or hardly any. And the solution to which I rallied in the end was to throw away all the stones but one, which I kept now in one pocket, now in another, and which of course I soon lost, or threw away, or gave away, or swallowed.

Beginning to End on American TV, 1971.

With Beckett's assistance, MacGowran pared tangential words and phrases, to make the tirades more cohesive for presentation — the "sucking stones" monologue, as written for *Molloy*, was eight pages long. Relentlessly, they carved the narrative to its essence, as the author himself had done consistently over the years, reworking the themes of his early novels into ever more concise fragments of theatre and prose.

At any length, the tongue-twisting structure of the monologues demanded an uncanny feat of memorization, perhaps more formidable than anything an actor of MacGowran's generation had ever tackled. Jack was almost paranoid about getting the words *right*, to an "and" and a "but"; it had to be absolutely correct at all times.

As MacGowran and Beckett fine-tuned their portrait of a man "striving for the ability to come to terms with death, and still to laugh at himself," they slowed down the pace of the material. Every syllable had to be crisp and distinct in its phrasing; the pauses etched between words were of no less importance than the words uttered between pauses.

"The dialogue was not naturalistic but Jack found the rhythm to it, which made it totally real," said Gordon Davidson, artistic director of the Mark Taper Forum in Los Angeles, where MacGowran later did the show. "Jack made me appreciate Beckett all the more; he made it so funny, so alive. Some actors bring things on a stage before the event happens, before they even open their mouths. I think Jack did that. All he had to do was put on that greatcoat, and it happened."

It happened first in Paris, in the spring of 1970, but it did not happen overnight. In MacGowran's hotel suite at the Pont-Royal, in the tiny Théâtre Édouard VII, in Beckett's cluttered apartment near the Gare Montparnasse where they had met so many times over the years, Jack and Sam spent hours and days and weeks editing, pacing, changing, arranging and rearranging the selections like so many sucking stones, until they fused them together to embody the many and varied facets of Beckett's vision.

Beginning with the opening pages of *Malone Dies* and concluding with the final words of *The Unnamable*, they created a seamless whole from the intercourse of their minds — a new *Beginning to End* that had evolved from the bastard marriage of mime and speech that marred *End of Day*, to a rich tapestry of words that evoked Beckett's sense of comic imagery and, above all, his compassion for the human condition.

Beckett himself directed the show, dedicating himself as wholly to the task as he had the creation of the words themselves. But he refused to take any credit for it; he had no desire to advance into MacGowran's spotlight, and he was too modest in any case.

KCET *Public Television*

"People find Beckett morose. I find him *so* funny."

Credit or no credit, Beckett was wholly in charge of the show. "Before he directs anything, Sam gets everyone together — every single person who has anything to do with the production," said Gloria MacGowran, who served as stage manager in Paris. "He talks to them, so that he has a team, and tells them what he's trying to do. If a line doesn't work, he'll change it or cut it. The only way Sam can find out how things work theatrically is to be there, to direct."

The author's theatrical sensibilities were sharp and distinct where they had once been tentative and imprecise. "His directions were deliberate and without a choice... He'd say, '*This* is the way *that* should go,' recalled MacGowran. "There were long pauses of silence while Beckett looked to the floor. Then he said two or three sentences and the whole thing was clear."

Beckett's quest for perfection extended to minute details. When Jack decided he had to have a boulder on the otherwise barren land-scape that was his stage, Sam and Gloria walked around Paris for two hours, looking for the precise color. Beckett finally found what he wanted in the step that led up to someone's house; he hired a man to construct the rock, showed him the step and gave him the dimensions. But neither Sam nor Jack were ever satisfied with it.

Beginning to End was accorded a typically rude welcome when it opened on April 23, 1970. Some patrons, like James Mason and Maggie Parker, were there to pay homage; others, including Salvador Dali and a large contingent of professional first-nighters and Parisian literati, were less respectful. They came for a laugh and talked all through the show.

Beckett, as per his custom, was nowhere to be seen during the performance. Instead he waited backstage with a warm embrace for his collaborator, his countryman and confrère. As usual, words between them were few. "Jack was like a brother," said Beckett later. "I didn't have to talk to him; I didn't have to direct him. He just *knew*."

11

The grey little fellow in the filthy black overcoat held his own at the Théâtre Édouard VII, despite the competition of the first-night audience. Rambling in comic exasperation and defiant rage, ambling from nostalgic recollection to bitter complaint, MacGowran poured forth every ounce of adrenalin he could muster. "Even if he had been the author he could not have shown greater conviction or fervor," observed writer-philosopher E.M. Cioran in *Le Monde*.

Describing the MacGowran-Beckett collaboration as "a lament for the living," Thomas Quinn Curtiss of *The New York Times* concluded that the show was open to various interpretations. "It might be a study of manic depression," he noted, "or a dramatization of Mark Twain's summing up of existence: 'When you're born, you're done for.'"

Beckett once again refused to elaborate on his work. He graciously posed for photographers and chatted with guests at a reception after the opening, but declined to make a statement. MacGowran had already squandered precious energy earlier in the day, talking at length with journalists, answering their every question; he had become Beckett's spokesman, on and off stage, and he was happy to oblige. But there were limits even to his patience.

An American woman living in Paris, who had managed to pass herself off as a playwright, was more persistent than most theatregoers. From the moment she saw *Beginning to End*, Gurney Campbell felt only one man could play Gandhi in her new play. MacGowran had long aspired to portray the beloved Hindu leader, whose philosophy and ideals had been a favorite topic of conversation in his Abbey days. But Campbell's script was an atrocity. It had a few good moments, but the moments were Gandhi's, not hers.

The playwright was determined that Jack accept the starring role in her latest "epic theatre" experiment. She pestered him incessantly despite his refusal to get involved. Only when she mentioned José Quintero as a potential director did MacGowran seriously consider the Off Broadway project.

He carefully weighed the elements. The salary wasn't much, but the role was choice; there were few men he more admired. Quintero had won great acclaim for his productions of Eugene O'Neill's plays; he could probably make the thing work if anyone could. But Campbell was no O'Neill, and *Gandhi* was no *Iceman Cometh*. The actor turned it down once more.

The producers, who figured the show would run for a year, then offered Jack more than twice as much money, as well as transportation for Gloria and Tara and an apartment in New York for all of them. MacGowran called Quintero to discuss the project. The director agreed the play needed major surgery; between the two of them, they finally decided they could make a success of it. MacGowran was also tired of collecting unemployment benefits, and so he accepted the job — after rejecting it four times.

The producers of *Beginning to End* meanwhile came up with a cockeyed scheme to transfer the show to Broadway in the fall of 1970. MacGowran and Beckett were wary of their intentions. The producers had quarreled amongst themselves and pulled their money out in Paris, before the last performance; Jack and Gloria had been forced to use their own funds to keep the theatre open, and were not reimbursed until months later.

Tom Parkinson threatened to sue MacGowran if he went ahead with *Gandhi*, which would conflict with the Beckett show. The producer claimed he had already set the New York dates, but remained vague when pressed for details. There was no contract and no agreement with Beckett. Parkinson was in no position to set up a production in New York, had no apparent funds and had made no effort to obtain a labor permit for MacGowran. The only thing he had was the unwieldy notion to stage the one-man show in Madison Square Garden.

MacGowran had read everything about Gandhi he could find by the time he sailed for New York in September. He even looked at old newsreels to learn how the man walked; the portrayal had to be accurate and true, down to the tiniest gesture. To his distress, he then discovered he and Gurney Campbell had a radically disparate point of view. He had nothing but respect for Gandhi; she utterly loathed him.

Worse yet the playwright usurped artistic control from José Quintero. She had invested her own money in the nearly four-hour show and would allow no alterations. *Gandhi* had 30 scenes taking place in nearly as many locales, jumping back in forth in time; a cast of 20 playing 34 roles; and a pair of inexperienced young producers — a financial consultant and a marketing executive — taking their first dip in the treacherous waters of New York theatre.

MacGowran knew the show needed a tremendous amount of work at the outset, but fully expected the problems to be worked out. He was disappointed in Quintero's inability to take charge and do what had to be done, to get rid of the clumsy narrative and keep the show moving. Some minor trimming at the last minute — on Jack's insistence — improved his part, but did not help the overall show.

"The biggest problem was that Campbell wouldn't cut the play," said actor Louis Guss, a veteran of many Quintero productions. "It had to be drastically cut and economized, and she thought every sentence was great. It was a history lesson rather than a drama. The play was too episodic; it never seemed to build or accumulate any tension."

After struggling through two and a half weeks of rehearsal, the director was ready to give up. "About a week before the opening José assembled the whole cast and said he was leaving the show. He told us he loved us all and hoped we'd have a success; it was a very emotional scene," recalled Guss. "Betty Miller [Mrs. Gandhi] practically begged him to stay. Quintero agreed to remain on the condition that Campbell did not interfere in any way."

MacGowran braved his way through the first performance, well aware they were on shaky ground. At the opening night party at Sardi's, he ran into his old pal Michael McAloney, who had helped him through the difficult period during *Juno*.

"What do you think, Mick? Do we have a chance?" he asked.

"You don't have a prayer," said McAloney. "If you're open tomorrow night, I'll be bloody amazed."

The next morning Gloria MacGowran opened *The New York Times* with great anxiety, only to learn that actor Patrick Wymark, a friend from Stratford days, was dead. She put the paper aside, then picked it up again and turned to the theatre page:

> Well intentioned, weak-minded and quite totally and unutterably boring, some kind of historical play, laughingly calling itself *Gandhi*, dragged its sluggard way into the Playhouse Theater last night. In the first place it is an insult to a great man, in the second place it is an insult to a great man, and in the third place it is a waste of another man who has many claims to being a great actor...
> — Clive Barnes, *The New York Times*, October 21, 1970

Jack and Gloria expected the show to limp on for a few days or a week, as a bad play would in London's West End. But the all powerful *Times* critic had delivered the coup de grâce. *Beginning to End* had survived a less-than-spectacular opening night to become one of the highlights of the Paris theatrical season; *Gandhi* never recovered from its première, nor did it deserve a second chance.

Word circulated in London that MacGowran had blacked his skin with a semi-permanent dye, and had to go to the Caribbean and blend

Photo by Bert Andrews

With Michael McAloney, at the opening night party for *Gandhi*.
New York, 1970.

in with the landscape until the dye wore off. Fortunately it was only a
rumor. There were others who believed the actor had fully expected
Gandhi to fail, and only used it as a vehicle to get to America.

But MacGowran did little dream that the biggest fiasco of his long
and erratic life in the theatre — the nadir of his and Quintero's respective careers — would make possible his crowning achievement. Even
before he awakened that day, three producers called the hotel, asking
him to reprise his one-man show.

MacGowran had thrown a copy of the Beckett script into his
suitcase on a whim. Now he and Gloria dug it out and made the rounds
of producers. The first engaged Jack in a cursory chat and told him to
have a look around the theatre while he kept an appointment with the
mayor; the second was quickly unsuitable.

Lastly they went to the Public Theater to see Joseph Papp. As they started to cross Lafayette Street, the actor realized he did not have his one and only copy of the script. He dashed up the street and chased the taxi to a stop, returning with the precious document.

The founder of the New York Shakespeare Festival had tried to get in touch with MacGowran years earlier, when he first heard the Claddagh recording of *MacGowran Speaking Beckett*, but he couldn't reach him. Later Jack was filming in Hong Kong when he got a wire asking him to bring the Beckett show to New York. But he had never heard of Papp and didn't take the offer too seriously; he doubted whether it would go over very well in America anyway.

MacGowran thought Beckett might be a writer of limited appeal in the United States, still a bit ahead of his time. But Papp convinced him otherwise. They adapted the show to suit the tiny stage of the Public's Newman Theater, and the youthful audiences that would fill it.

The actor loved the young people, the awestruck students who had flocked to see the show in Paris. They were so open-minded and aware, so eager to understand; they knew exactly what he was doing. MacGowran wanted to make Beckett accessible to everyone, but inside he felt it was for the young.

Joe Papp, who had found the actor "disarmingly gentle" on their first meeting, was overwhelmed by MacGowran's enthusiasm and cooperation during rehearsal. "I was directing the show at first," he remembered. "I asked Jack about something: 'Would you mind trying it this way?' And he did it, just like that. I thought, 'I'd better be careful — he'll do anything.' He understood the gloom, and the life force of the material. I didn't want to interfere; he had his own sense of direction.

"The tiniest things meant a lot to Jack — simple things — he was very precise about his makeup, very exacting about the size of the rock. He didn't permit anything to go against the nature of the character," said Papp. "The slightest thing that happened on the stage was of extreme importance to him — it was a total organic thing. The blocking, the pauses, all the little movements that would normally be 'stage traffic' — with Jack it was never just stage traffic, it was an art."

Despite the rapport of actor and producer, there was some question as to whether MacGowran would be able to do the show. Actor's Equity had ruled that a foreigner — even a star — could not come to the U.S. for a play, and then do another when it folded. Six months had to pass inbetween, which meant the cost of living would force Jack and his family to leave.

There was one exception to the rule, however. If no other actor could play the role, he might be allowed to do it. Papp wrote a letter to that effect, enabling MacGowran to stay in New York, and Beckett cabled his express permission for Jack to perform the show. When an Off Broadway strike further threatened the project, Papp agreed to stage the show under a regular Broadway production contract.

Ming Cho Lee, who had constructed an imaginative maze of ramps, platforms and bridges for *Gandhi*, did the set design for the Public Theater. Lee created a desolate wilderness of strange, cosmic-like swirls, keeping in mind Jack's desire that the stage suggest a womb; in Paris, the backdrop had depicted a fertilized ovum.

If the set had precisely the look and the feel he wanted, Beckett's avatar was distressed by his own appearance. He had shaved his head to play Gandhi and what he saw in the mirror was not at all his idea of the Beckett protagonist, with the wild, disheveled hair. Papp tried five different wigs on him; none of them looked right. MacGowran finally made a transatlantic call to Beckett and asked for his opinion.

"I think probably the tramp could have been bald because of lice or something," the author observed. Only with Beckett's reassurance that his stubbly head was in character was Jack satisfied, as Sam's approval was critical to him at all times.

He was at home with his long, thin face — the pouches beneath his eyes, the creases in his brow, the puffy jowls, the scarred and blistered lips — and he knew how to use it to his advantage. He blended the makeup in his hands and applied it with the utmost care, accentuating the lines he already had, drawing in shadows for emphasis. It took an hour, sometimes an hour and a half, and then he required solitude.

In preparing for an ordinary play, Jack did not have the need to be alone. But the Beckett show brought him to the theatre far in advance of his performance so he could relax and concentrate, "get the whole show, more or less, in a relaxed frame of mind."

Jack MacGowran in the Works of Samuel Beckett opened November 19, 1970, under the auspices of the New York Shakespeare Festival. The actor's agent, Robert Lantz, was enthralled by the show, but unsure about the limits of its appeal. "In the present economic difficulties in this country and in this city, it is difficult to know whether there is enough of an audience to sustain a one-man show of this kind, but certainly it should be successful," he wrote his London counterpart, Maggie Parker. "Everything will depend not only on the reviews, but most specifically the review in *The New York Times*."

Lantz's worries proved ill-founded when Mel Gussow called the evening "pure and perfect" in the morning paper and described MacGowran as "the quintessential Beckett actor." He continued:

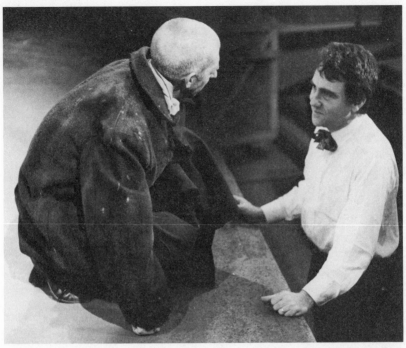

Courtesy of Joseph Papp

Staging the Beckett show in New York with producer Joseph Papp.

For people who know Beckett the show will be an absolute pleasure; for those who do not, it will be something of a revelation. Author and actor are so commonly rooted in spirit that if Beckett were an actor he would be MacGowran, if MacGowran were a writer he would be Beckett. It is an exact meeting of author and role such as one seldom finds in a play, and almost never finds in a one-man show. This is not just a reading, or an impersonation, but an incarnation of the work and of the man... It is an evening in the presence of two consummate artists exactly in tune with each other.

— *The New York Times*, November 20, 1970

Clive Barnes later that week praised the show as strongly as he had damned the actor's previous vehicle. "I urge anyone interested in the theatre or in the nature of man — and I suppose it should be the same interest — to go immediately to see Mr. MacGowran play Beckett," he advocated, encouraging his readers to "see it, embrace it."

Harold Clurman observed in *The Nation*, "I shall never again be able to think of Samuel Beckett's writing without associating it with the face, the flesh, the voice, the posture of Jack MacGowran... one of the truly important actors of our day."

In a broader appeal to the man on the street, John Schubeck of WABC TV enthusiastically told his vast television audience: "What Nathan did for the hot dog, MacGowran does for Beckett."

The New York critics were virtually unanimous in their opinion of the show, trumpeting its arrival on U.S. soil with the roar and thunder of their approval. Beckett himself uncharacteristically reveled in the glory:

> The news of your marvellous success in N.Y. is the best for many a long day. Bravo bravissimo... I imagine you will be getting fat offers right left and centre after this and probably staying on in the States for a time. After all your hard work and difficulties and disappointments I truly am delighted for you and Gloria and for myself.
> — Letter to MacGowran, December 12, 1970

Less delighted was a friend who recalled the 1965 Dublin production. "The one in New York was much slicker. It had the visual aspect of being deliberately staged," said Tom Clancy. "The show was rough in Dublin, but it was much more personal. It was in a very small theatre — you felt you were right there with Beckett."

Jack himself was not quite satisfied with either performance. But then he never was, despite the plaudits garnered. He hated going to pictures he'd done, seeing himself on the screen. He despised long runs in the theatre, and often played with the interpretation of a line to keep himself amused. Not on stage and not in films did he ever feel he had done his best; only in *Eh Joe* on BBC Television, under Beckett's direction, was he wholly pleased with his work.

If *MacGowran in the Works of Beckett* was a show that made great and unusual demands on the theatregoer — regardless of his familiarity with the author — it made far greater demands on the performer. MacGowran awoke one Saturday morning in mid-December to find himself completely out of voice. A doctor diagnosed the problem as "vocal fatigue" and ordered him to rest for three days; four performances were cancelled. He went on again Tuesday night but found himself in trouble the next morning. The doctor warned if he did not rest for a least a week, he could do himself permanent injury.

MacGowran did six performances a week instead of eight when he returned to the Public Theater. But it was Gloria who had to tell Joe

As Beckett's Everyman in the triumphant 1970 New York Shakespeare
Festival production of *Jack MacGowran in the Works of Samuel Beckett.*

Papp that he couldn't do it eight times a week, that it was simply too much for him. He would never admit it himself.

"Jackie had a marvelous stubborness. No matter what he was feeling like, he would get up on that stage and do what he was expected to do. It was that stubborness that got him through those early, difficult days," said actress Billie Whitelaw. "Before you can do Beckett in any way, you *have* to have a sense of stubborness. It's rather like wrestling with an octopus; you have to take the octopus and win."

One word, above all, was missing from MacGowran's vocabulary. *Failure.* Mastering the requisite mental gymnastics of the show was a resolution of mind over matter; the unbridled energy Jack forced onto the stage was a matter of mind over body. But time was working against him; the aging process he had once held at bay had finally caught up with him. All appearance of youth he had retained well into his forties had vanished, and his physical decline grew ever rapid.

12

MacGowran sought constant assurance from those around him toward the end of his life. He needed protection from the outside world; he couldn't tolerate the company of people for very long unless they were close friends. Few realized how sad he was, or knew he was a manic-depressive.

"Acting was an all-consuming thing with Jack; nothing else mattered. It's hard to survive that way," said Joseph Papp. "His body was a total instrument, he had no defenses. Jack was like litmus paper; everything left a mark on him, or a bruise."

If the finer details had slipped by unnoticed during the years MacGowran spent in an alcoholic fog, the unfairness of life had not. The petty squabbles, the imagined slights, the great injustices and the bitter memory of it all ate at his intestines like a cancer.

Beckett gave MacGowran the words to express what he felt deep within. Jack didn't have the guts to say such things himself, but as an actor he could give voice to them — and get away with it. Malone and all the other Beckett protagonists spoke for *him*:

Let me say before I go any further that I forgive nobody. I wish them all an atrocious life and then the fires and ice of hell and in the execrable generations to come an honoured name.

The actor had worked himself into a state of exhaustion by the time *MacGowran in the Works of Beckett* closed on January 24, 1971, after 61 performances. Papp wanted MacGowran to do a year's run, but agent Robert Lantz put his foot down. The show was too demanding and too strenuous to be played en suite; the throat trouble was a warning to be heeded, not ignored.

Those who were unaware of the situation sought only to increase his burden. The Graduate School of Social Work at New York University had assigned the show as homework; they invited MacGowran to come and study "the impact of [his] performance on graduate students training to be social workers." Jack was forced to turn down all such offers during the run. His agents often had to decline for him after he had accepted.

Rosette Lamont, who taught a course devoted to Beckett at the City

KCET *Public Television*

The words were Beckett's, the anguish MacGowran's.

University of New York, was one of many whose requests were denied. But her motivations, unlike others, were not altogether selfish. "By speaking to an intellectual group, Mr. MacGowran will reach the very people who can appreciate him, and spread his fame," she told Jack's agent. "I know he himself is too modest a person to think in such terms; that is why we must do so for him."

MacGowran was indeed too modest to entertain such thoughts. He was contemptuous of actors who sold themselves as goods. There was talk of an Academy Award nomination for Best Supporting Actor when Peter Brook's *King Lear* was released that year, but it never got beyond talk. Far less gifted performers had politicked and promoted themselves to the hilt for an Oscar; Jack never dreamed of hiring a press agent, or lifting a finger in self-endorsement.

When Maggie Parker learned that David Lean was planning a film on Gandhi, she touted MacGowran as the perfect candidate for the part — he had received glowing notices for his stage portrayal, despite the play's failure. But Jack had not forgotten *Doctor Zhivago*; he told his London agent he would have nothing to do with Lean. Parker knew what the film would mean in terms of prestige and remuneration, however, and continued to promote him for the role — first to Lean, who eventually dropped the project, and then to Richard Attenborough, who would struggle for years to get it on the screen.

MacGowran lost out on two film offers which did appeal to him, as a result of his commitment to Beckett and Papp. He was forced to turn down Roman Polanski's adaptation of *Macbeth* at the outset of his Off Broadway run; he also forfeited a leading role in a German film project, which he had won on Beckett's personal recommendation.

But the spectacular reviews he received for the one-man show brought forth many more offers in the next few months. Alan Schneider wanted Jack to play Vladimir in a 12-to-16 week U.S. tour of *Waiting for Godot*. A man who said Beckett had given him the film rights to *Act Without Words I* was anxious to obtain the actor's services. And there were two proposals from Los Angeles to record *MacGowran in the Works of Beckett* for posterity; one from a documentary filmmaker and the other from a non-commercial television station.

Jack was tired of repeating things he had already done. Few of the offers appealed to him, old or new, and those that did were often economically unfeasible. He turned down Schneider's "ridiculous" offer to tour in *Godot*, but agreed to do *Krapp's Last Tape* under his direction for TV. Jack had passed up the chance to play Krapp on BBC TV a decade earlier, out of loyalty to Patrick Magee; it was *his* play.

MacGowran was intrigued by Joe Papp's suggestion that he play

King Lear, but he was hardly ready to take on such an arduous stage role. Nor was he really of a mind to take on anything other than the Beckett show. Jack identified with the characters he played in any circumstance, but he understood and felt with Beckett's Everyman on a deeper and more intimate plane than most people imagined. He wore the greatcoat like a second skin; even in the sweltering heat of the California desert during a TV taping of the show, when temperatures rose to over 100°, he could not part with the costume between takes.

"Jackie became so engrossed in Beckett, you couldn't draw him out of himself," said Siobhán McKenna, who was in New York with her own one-woman show. "But then you'd mention something, and his face would light up — as if you'd reminded him of the person he'd been, before he became so totally absorbed in the work."

MacGowran's devotion to Beckett paid unexpected dividends. Neither he nor Joe Papp were prepared for the reception to the show, the success and adulation. Jack was staggered by the prestigious Obie award for Best Actor in an Off Broadway performance, and the accolades that followed. The Drama Desk award, the *Variety* Poll of New York drama critics and the Critic's Circle award were wholly unforeseen, but not unwelcome.

Invitations to do the one-man show poured in from every corner of the globe. Colleges and universities, cultural organizations, theatre festival organizers and self-styled entrepreneurs deluged MacGowran, asking him to bring the show to Zurich, Berlin, Montreal and Papua New Guinea, to London, Rome and San Juan. Even Hollywood made overtures to him, and not to play "a little green man."

Premio Roma, the international festival of performing arts in Rome, offered MacGowran $1250 for a single performance of the Beckett program. The deal fell through when the festival could not afford to pick up his travel expenses. The offer from Beirut was more typical — in spirit, if not specifics — of the many he received: "no money, just expenses."

Jack could no longer work in England — where he owed £7000 in back taxes — and was forced to turn down an invitation to appear at Reading University, in conjunction with a major Beckett exhibition. But he had no desire to do the show in London, where he felt neither he nor Beckett were fully appreciated.

MacGowran took the Beckett show to Washington, D.C., and then embarked on a tour of the U.S. that took him to Harvard and Princeton, and other universities in and around New England. The itinerary was poorly organized; he was forced to travel back and forth in an illogical pattern with no regard for distance between engagements.

On location in the Mojave desert for American TV, with producer Lewis Freedman.

On paper, the Beckett tour was a triumph. Financially, it was a washout — like all of his artistic successes. In New York Jack had received $350 a week against 10% of the box office, plus 2% of the gross for his adaptation; on the road he contracted for $2500 a week plus 5% of the tour company's receipts. But after guild fees, agent's commissions, traveling expenses for his family and taxes there was virtually nothing left. When Beckett heard about MacGowran's financial woes, he asked Grove Press to give the actor $2000 out of his royalties.

The actor's agent was inundated with offers for him, while he was on tour. A New York publisher wanted to know if he would consider writing a biography of Beckett. Joe Papp asked him to do *Much Ado About Nothing* in Central Park. José Quintero wanted him to reprise *Hughie* on television. Jack agreed to co-star in a film with Richard Burton, but writer-director Wolf Mankowitz was unable to finance the project.

While he could have made substantially more by accepting some of the film and television offers that came his way, MacGowran remained on tour. The college students had an insatiable appetite for Beckett, and their hunger kept him going, above all else. "They know what I'm doing," he said, "though I can't stand the intellectuals who come backstage and drive me batty looking for meanings in Beckett that simply do not exist. They're looking for symbols that just aren't there."

Gloria did her best to shield Jack from the highbrows who wanted to discuss Beckett's symbolism, and the casual "buddies" who came backstage, but she could not keep him from his adoring fans. Even when he was completely drained, he granted them an audience and played the gracious host.

One backstage visitor, who was awed by his performance, observed, "It was more his talent as a man that struck me. He possessed the rare gift of recognizing, accepting and drawing out the human qualities of others," said aspiring actress Cathy Lynch. "I witnessed it when several of his friends dropped by the dressing room and when a stage-struck girl read him a poem she'd written. When his friends came in, no one was more important than anyone else — at that moment, we were all his friends. And he listened to a long, strangled poem which was beautiful only to its author, and he saw that beauty because Jack MacGowran obviously cared."

It was a quality MacGowran shared with Beckett, whose state of mind he knew intimately. He credited his remarkable friendship with the author as the sole source of his ability to choreograph Beckett's spare, cerebral poetry into a vibrant ballet. "I know what Beckett thinks, I know his way of life. I know when he's happy, I know when he's not happy," Jack observed. "I might be feeling a bit under, and not showing it, and Sam would know; he would know immediately because he's a very kind man. He's taken many a human being out of the wilderness and put him on the straight road — Sam is built that way. He loves doing this for people, because he loves people — genuinely."

It was not an intellectual affinity MacGowran had with Beckett but a spiritual affinity. Jack understood Sam in a visceral way he could not articulate, in spite of his attempts. Neither need make explanations to the other; to communicate they hardly need speak.

But MacGowran found himself speaking *for* Beckett, offstage as well as on, with increasing frequency as he toured. Where the author would not or could not elucidate on his writing, Jack took pleasure in discussing both the work and the man. But while he expounded on Beckett in interviews and lectures, his knowledge of the subject was best stated in performance.

"I would listen to him talk sometimes and think, 'You don't have the faintest idea of what you're talking about," said Donald McWhinnie. "Jackie was not an intellect at all. He was an instinctive human being, this was the great thing about him. That's what made him a great actor."

MacGowran had made a name for himself in the decade since he had first performed *End of Day* under McWhinnie's direction, and his visit to the 1972 Dublin Theatre Festival was duly celebrated. The Beckett show was the culmination of all his dreams and struggles, and the Irish conferred their Actor of the Year award upon him.

In his later years MacGowran found it increasingly difficult to return to the dingy, parochial town on the banks of the River Liffey that claimed him as a native son. While he was met always by great love and affection, he sensed that some of his former associates resented his success; many were still tied to the Abbey or the Gate, with little to show for the years since he had exiled himself from their midst.

"I still consider myself very much a Dubliner, but I have in a small way what Joyce had, a love-hate relationship with the city," MacGowran admitted. "I love it because I know it so well; I hate it because I know it so well. If you want to join the pub set, the if-I-were-a-king set, everybody is happy because you are no longer a threat to anybody. If you become a threat in your profession you arouse enmity and the city and its people turn on you."

The actor's triumph turned sour when he unwisely chose to follow his one-man show at the Gaiety Theatre with *The Caretaker* in May. He had reportedly passed up Pinter for Shakespeare when asked to tour with the play in 1960, and he had always regretted the decision.

MacGowran ran into difficulty early in rehearsal when he found himself struggling to memorize the lines — a problem he had never experienced. Harold Pinter's dialogue, while clearly showing the influence of Beckett, seemed largely aimless and repetitious by comparison; it had none of his favorite writer's wit and lyricism, nor his economy of language.

The role of Davies, a homeless vagabond, also presented a problem. MacGowran had no desire to emulate Donald Pleasence, who had created the part, but he was unable to supress his vivid recollection of the British actor's highly charged and highly acclaimed portrayal. Worse yet, another character discussed electroshock treatments similar to ones Jack had been given for depression, and Pinter's graphic description of them teased and tormented MacGowran.

The day he was scheduled to open in the play, he paid an ill-timed call on his elderly mother. "You're nothing but a failure," she told him during the visit. "You're just like your father; you'll never amount to anything."

MacGowran sank into an almost suicidal despair. Her unprovoked attack cut him deep, just when he was most in need of an encouraging word. It was a hellish opening night, and he looked like death by the time he took his curtain call.

Nigel Anthony and Frank Barrie, the two young actors who shared the stage with Jack, could have easily taken advantage of him. But they felt he was due a certain respect, and they helped him through a difficult run. The play was scheduled for three weeks but pulled after the second. Jack began to fear he was losing his memory; Gloria pushed him back into the one-man show for a week to restore his confidence, though the program had run its course. MacGowran survived *The Caretaker*, but to experience such a dismal personal failure — in his hometown, on the heels of his great success — was the beginning of the end.

Jack and Gloria recuperated from the ordeal in the tranquil mountains of County Wicklow, at the estate of their friend, Garech Browne. The actor had sufficiently regained his equilibrium by the time he returned to the States in July, to do the Beckett show at a festival in Chicago, but he was still low on energy.

Job offers were plentiful, as well as predictable. Princeton University asked MacGowran to reprise *Endgame* with Pat Magee, under Beckett's direction. Irish Arts in Toronto wanted to reunite Jack and Siobhán McKenna, in *Juno and the Paycock*; they also asked Jack to star in and direct three of W.B. Yeats' one-act plays. New York's Lincoln Center sought him for the role of Fluther Good in a revival of *The Plough and the Stars*.

Beckett, MacGowran and Magee were all agreeable to staging the definitive *Endgame* in America — provided the rehearsals took place in Paris — but they couldn't come to terms with the university. Jack was less excited about the prospect of doing either of the O'Casey plays yet again. He leaned slightly in favor of Toronto, where his old pal Sean Kenny was set to direct, but he didn't really want to accept either offer; he was exhausted, and tired of O'Casey altogether.

When William Friedkin asked MacGowran to play a film director in *The Exorcist* that fall, he readily agreed. Jack's agent felt it would be a good *commercial* launching pad to follow up the prestige of the one-man show; the actor found horror movies terribly amusing in general, and was fascinated with the story of a child possessed by the devil.

MacGowran found the financial arrangements even more attractive. His contract with Warner Bros. promised a salary of $2,000 a week, though he ultimately worked only 17 days over a period of 11 weeks. For once in his life he had a chance to make a little money, and

With Garech Browne of Claddagh Records, at a reception in Dublin.

he was unembarrassed by it. Jack had never cared about money, had no concept of money — when he had it, he spent it — but he had a wife and daughter, and he was concerned with their welfare.

As it turned out, neither Irish Arts nor the Lincoln Center Repertory Company were willing to take no for an answer. MacGowran could portray O'Casey's wise fools better than any actor of his generation — when he wasn't playing Beckett's sad clowns — and his potential employers both felt they *had* to have him. He managed to get out of playing Joxer in *Juno and the Paycock*, despite premature announcements of his participation. But he was eventually pushed into doing *The Plough and the Stars* when his defenses were down: Gloria had returned to Ireland and was not around to say no.

Before MacGowran could step into Fluther's hobnail boots, there was the problem of his commitment to Warner Bros., which complicated matters greatly. "I was very upset when the studio said no," recalled Jules Irving, director at Lincoln Center. "I felt so strongly about having Jack in the play, I agreed to arrange my rehearsal schedule so he would be on first call to Billy Friedkin. Billy loved the idea of seeing the play, and of seeing Jack in it, so there was a deal made; he brought it about."

MacGowran based his portrayal of the mock-heroic Fluther partly on pub pal Brendan Behan; he also found elements of Beckett's Vladimir creeping in. The fact that he was filming *The Exorcist* during the day and rehearsing *The Plough* in the evening did not compromise the integrity of the performance — nor did the fact that he hated doing the show. Jack would have preferred the role of the Young Covey, if he had to do the O'Casey play again; the producers, however, felt he was too old for the part.

The actor's familiarity with the play was so great that the youthful director in charge had trouble projecting his own point of view. "Jackie was always very deferential toward me, as I was with him," said Dan Sullivan. "And yet there was a clash there, maybe in terms of age; I'm not sure what it was. He had this tempo which sometimes drove me nuts. There was no way of speeding him up. We never got into a confrontation about it because I realized very early there was no way I could change it; it was MacGowran's rhythm and it stayed exactly the same."

Yet his young director held him in high regard. "I always sensed the thing that made him work as a performer was his rage, that incredible rage inside that funny little body. There was something boiling up in that frame all the time — you could see what a Covey he must've been, the rage that he had. MacGowran was *the* loudest actor I've ever heard. He could make more noise, that little guy — his entire body must have been a resonator," observed Sullivan. "*Jeezus*, he was amazing."

He was, however, mortal. On a chilly December day, as MacGowran walked briskly down the street, a sharp sudden pain stabbed at his chest. For a moment the pressure was so intense he could scarcely breathe.

A doctor out on Long Island determined that the trouble was neither a heart attack nor a cracked rib this time. It was an angina condition. The arteries had become hardened through years of abuse; they were unable to deliver sufficient oxygen to the heart muscles. It was nature's way of telling MacGowran to slow down, that the heart had been overworked.

"It's the type of disease for which by-pass surgery is done these days," stated Dr. Daniel Sheehan, who made the diagnosis. "It came at a bad time for Jack. He didn't want to get into it or face it, that the angina might be a problem. I told him, 'It's not a thing you shrug off when somebody tells you.' But he made light of it. I suggested he call

With director William Friedkin on the set of *The Exorcist*, late in 1972.

his doctor in London and discuss it with him. Jack didn't appear to be interested in having any further investigation of it."

Neither hangover or exhaustion had ever stopped MacGowran from fulfilling his commitments, and the sudden incidence of angina was not allowed to interfere with his work. William Friedkin turned out to be almost as much of a perfectionist as Roman Polanski, with the result that *The Exorcist* went considerably over schedule; MacGowran's chores lasted through the third week of December, overlapping with dress rehearsals for the play.

The Plough and the Stars opened at the Vivian Beaumont Theater on January 4. It was more a triumph for Jack than the company as a whole:

> Mr. MacGowran prances with a graveyard reverence, and clowns with sadness. His acting is a constant joy. The play itself proves a more fitful experience.
> — Clive Barnes, *The New York Times*, January 5, 1973

If he dazzled the opening night audience with his usual effervescence, MacGowran's friends and associates began to sense a gradual decline in him during the run of the play. Jack was 54 years old and his erratic lifestyle was finally catching up with him; he was no longer able to hide his fatigue from those around him.

"There was something spent in him. That drive, that vitality wasn't there," asserted actor Michael Clarke-Laurence, who served as dialogue consultant. "A lot of damage had been done to that machine. Jack was brilliant as Fluther, but there was a wavering concentration that was totally unlike him, a loss of energy and dynamism he always had. I saw him missing lines he knew."

Words that were close to him would not come, and he began to falter in his always quick, light-footed movements. His flawless sense of timing started to slide. Before long, Jack found himself missing cues; he would forget where he was and wander off.

MacGowran never discussed his problems with anyone and even, at times, denied them to himself. But he could not shrug off the cumulative exhaustion, nor the recurring chest pains, as easily as he had once dismissed the effects of too much alcohol.

The pains, in particular, were an awful bother; he simply didn't have time for them. As soon as the show closed on February 10, the actor would attend to some personal business in Dublin; he would also go to Los Angeles for a prearranged meeting with his idol, James Cagney. Then he would take the one-man show to Toronto, Montreal and Rome. That summer he would do the Beckett program at the Guthrie Theater in Minneapolis, where he was slated to direct his own production of *Juno and the Paycock* as well. And there were a number of film roles in the offing.

Eileen O'Casey had lunch with the actor at the Russian Tea Room one day and found him depressed. "We went for a long walk, and we talked about Sean and the old days in Torquay," remembered the playwright's widow. "Jack said he was tired, and he really didn't care much what happened. I said, 'But you've got all this work coming.' He was happy about that for Gloria and Tara, but for himself he didn't care — he was really despondent."

Later that week, on Friday, January 26, MacGowran came down with the London flu and was forced to leave the cast of *The Plough*. He was confined to bed in his twelfth floor suite at the storied Algonquin Hotel, and missed the weekend performances.

With the aid of a long overdue rest, and a continuous flow of tea and soup from the hotel kitchen, Jack began to feel better. On Monday, he insisted he was going to rejoin the show. The actor honestly didn't feel well enough to go back to work; his face was pale, his body aching. He wanted to return only because he had been so unreliable in his drinking days — he was afraid the producers would think he was "up to his old tricks."

Gloria agreed with the doctor — it was too soon for Jack to return. But he was adamant about rejoining the show Tuesday. "I feel bloody marvelous," he told an associate on the phone. "I'll be back tomorrow."

That night MacGowran sat up in bed chatting happily with Gloria and his stepdaughter, Melanie Carvill. They made some coffee and talked on into the early morning hours. Jack was laughing and talking about man-eating sharks and spearfishing in Australia, where he had filmed *Age of Consent*. It was not the laughter of a man who cared little for family life, a fatigued and embittered man who had forgotten how to enjoy life, but that of a young and thirsty Irish lad with all the world before him.

Suddenly he said, "I feel very tired, darlings." MacGowran took a heavy breath. He laid his head back on the pillow and closed his eyes.

"He's dead," said Gloria.

"No, he isn't," said Melanie.

Photo by Martha Swope

The parting glass: Jack MacGowran in his last role, as Fluther Good in
O'Casey's *The Plough and the Stars*. Kevin Conway and Leo Leyden are in
the background. New York, 1973.

Epilogue

A great burden was lifted from Jack MacGowran's shoulders as the dawn rose over Manhattan on January 30, 1973. The suffering and the pain had ended; he was finally at peace. The cause of death — widely attributed to the flu — was the angina he had sought to ignore.

His restless searching and deprivation had carried him to the threshold of international stardom. It was ironic that he would die, just as he was beginning to come into his own. But he was free at last, of his overwhelming burden, and it gave his family solace.

The company at Lincoln Center fell into a state of shock when they got the word. "The warning signs were there," said Dan Sullivan, "but somehow they went unnoticed. It was the fullness of his nature being cut short — he was there giving very full performances. That vitality obviously had to have been manufactured at great expense."

That night, during a performance dedicated to Jack's memory, a line of Fluther's gave the cast a jolt:

It's only a little cold I have; there's nothing derogatory wrong with me.

When Samuel Beckett heard the news, he immediately contacted Barney Rosset at Grove Press and asked him to take $2,000 from royalty monies and deliver it to Gloria. In death, as in life, he understood and provided for Jack's needs without a word being uttered.

MacGowran could not have known the effect he had on Beckett, or on other friends and associates, the way that he touched their hearts and minds. He was unaware of the childlike innocence he projected that made audiences immediately sympathetic to him; he was too modest to imagine how much he was loved by those who loved him, and how much they would miss him.

Few who knew the quiet, gentle soul were able to accept the fact that he was gone. Billie Whitelaw, who was in London performing *Not I* — which Beckett had written for her — looked to her departed friend for strength and reassurance. "Every night before that curtain went up, I used to say, 'Right, MacGowran, spread your wings and start flying down, please. Help is needed.' To me, Jackie's not dead," said Whitelaw. "I love him dearly, and I can't take his death seriously at all."

A memorial service was held on February 1, at Campbell's funeral parlor in New York. The service started precisely at 11:30 a.m. Joseph Papp offered a brief tribute at Gloria's request. He eulogized the actor as "a gentle soul buffeted about by life," and closed with Clov's last words from *Endgame*:

> ...I open the door of the cell and go. I am so bowed I only see my feet, if I open my eyes, and between my legs a little trail of black dust. I say to myself that the earth is extinguished, though I never saw it lit. It's easy going. When I drop I'll weep for happiness.

The service lasted all of five minutes. The Irish contingent were horrified; they had come for a wake. "Jesus," whispered Dublin actor Patrick Bedford to his colleagues. "They shoved our poor bloody friend into the fuckin' ground pretty fast, didn't they?"

But Gloria MacGowran did not want a wake or a long, drawn out funeral. She wanted it simple. Jack had always hated funerals and she knew he would have hated to participate in a long one himself.

MacGowran had lived and breathed Beckett, and he wanted to be with him at the end. He was cremated at his request; Joe Papp and Robbie Lantz saw to it that his ashes were taken out by helicopter and scattered over the sea, in accordance with Gloria's wishes, so that a part of him might drift throughout the world. Beckett provided her the means to convey the actor on his final journey, in a passage in *From an Abandoned Work*:

> Just under the surface I shall be, all together at first, then separate and drift, through all the earth and perhaps in the end through a cliff *into the sea, something of me.*

Notes and Sources

Firsthand interviews with Jack MacGowran's friends and associates constituted the primary research for this book. MacGowran's personal scrapbooks and clipping files provided much information, particularly about the beginnings of his career in Dublin; they were placed at my disposal by Gloria MacGowran, as were the files of his agent, Robert Lantz, which afforded an invaluable behind-the-scenes look at the latter part of MacGowran's career. The scrapbooks of the Dublin Gate Theatre, now housed at Northwestern University Library, Evanston, Illinois, helped to further document the Dublin years.

Additional background information was gleaned from the pages of *The Times* of London, *The Sunday Times, The Irish Independent, The Sunday Independent, The Irish Times, The Irish Press, The Guardian, The Evening Standard, The New York Times, The New Yorker, The Washington Post, Variety, The Hollywood Reporter, Modern Drama, Screen World, Theatre World, Stagecast, International Theatre Annual*, and *Who's Who in the Theatre*.

Samuel Beckett's letters to Jack MacGowran are on deposit at the Harry Ransom Humanities Research Center, University of Texas, Austin. Beckett's letters to Alan Schneider first appeared in *The Village Voice*, March 19, 1958, and are reprinted in Samuel Beckett, *Disjecta: Miscellaneous Writings and a Dramatic Fragment*, ed. Ruby Cohn (London: John Calder, 1983).

PROLOGUE

13   ...submerge in alcohol. Gloria MacGowran to JY, June 22, 1975-June 5, 1979; Melanie Carvill to JY, May 21-29, 1975.

13   One day in Philadelphia... Gloria MacGowran to JY.

14   "...clapping my hands..." Samuel Beckett, *Malone Dies*, in *Three Novels*, p.243.

16   One night in Washington... Danny McCarthy to JY, May 21, 1975; Jack MacGowran to Winfred Blevins, *The Los Angeles Herald-Examiner*, February 13, 1971.

18   "I don't want anyone..." Gloria MacGowran to JY. With Beckett's approval, Dublin actor Barry McGovern put together a one-man show entitled *I'll Go On* in 1984, using different selections from the author's novels.

18   "...I'll go on." *The Unnamable*, in *Three Novels*, p. 577.

CHAPTER 1

19   "I was born when I met Sam..." Jack MacGowran, autobiographical fragment, circa 1972 (unpublished).

20   ...quell the rebellion. Michael McAloney to JY, January 21, 1975.

20   ...a gun in the child's face. Rita Darragh and Mamie Hamilton to JY, July 17, 1975.

21   It was in Tommy... E.L. Carew to JY, July 14, 1975; Darach Connolly, Bob Casey to JY, July 19, 1975.

22   "...called upon to perform." Benedict Daly to JY, July 19, 1975.
22   "...no training at all." Dick O'Rafferty to JY, July 9, 1975.
23   "...most profound influence." *The Irish Independent,* January 10, 1965.
24   "...spontaneously into the dialog." Brendan Smith to JY, July 19, 1975.
25   "...saved our bacon for that." Hilton Edwards to JY, July 10, 1975.
26   "...fortune for both of us." Gabriel Fallon to JY, July 8, 1975.
26   "...hard way, and Jackie did." Stanley Illsley to JY, July 11, 1975.
27   "...gone into his own world." Eamonn Andrews to JY, September 22, 1975.
27   "...stick out the hard times." Seamus Kelly to JY, October 16, 1975.
27   ...simply ignored him. Siobhán McKenna to JY, October 26, 1975.
28   "...first discovered him." *The Evening Standard,* January 24, 1947.

CHAPTER 2

29   Jack completed his paper... Gloria MacGowran to JY.
30   ..."wear the man down." MacGowran to Des Hickey and Gus Smith, *A Paler Shade of Green.*
30   "...back up." Harry Brogan to JY, August 28, 1975.
32   "...honorable thing to do." Grania O'Shannon to JY, June 16, 1975.
32   ...and his only love. MacGowran, "Jack MacGowran."
32   "...short of summary execution." Ronnie Walsh to JY, October 20, 1975.
33   "...and then walk home." Micheál Ó Briain to JY, July 23, 1975.
33   "...down to a small thing." Paddy Dooley to JY, July 23, 1975.
34   There were times... Tomás Mac Anna to JY, July 16, 1975; Micheál Ó Briain to JY.
34   "...an extraordinary gift." Michael Clarke-Laurence to JY, May 26, 1975.
34   ...standard Abbey fare. MacGowran to JY, February 13, 1972.
34   Jack Yeats became... Grania O'Shannon to JY; Brian O'Higgins to JY, July 27, 1975.
35   ...pleased him immeasurably. Jack B. Yeats to MacGowran, letter, April 20, 1949.
35   As MacGowran immersed himself... MacGowran, Preface to *In Sand.*
35   "I hope I have succeeded..." Ibid.
36   "...damage to the parent Abbey." MacGowran to JY.
36   "...our so-called naturalism." Ibid.
37   "...It was overdone." Dick O'Rafferty to JY.
37   "...every actor in the world." *The Sunday Times,* February 6, 1966.
37   "...parts for Indian peddlers." Gloria MacGowran to JY. There are many variations on this story, which has become a legend in Dublin acting circles.

CHAPTER 3

38   "...searchings and deprivation." Ronnie Walsh to JY.
38   "...circumstances around him." Eddie Golden to JY, July 23, 1975.
38   ...wanted to be an original. Concepta Fennell to JY, January 8, 1979.
39   Ford had made a handshake... Maureen O'Hara to JY, November 19, 1976.
40   One night after a round... Gloria MacGowran to JY.
40   *...fall on my face.* Billie Whitelaw to JY, July 1, 1975.

42 "...spoiled it for him." Dick O'Rafferty to JY.
42 "...elaborately prepared." Richard Pine, *All for Hecuba*.
43 "..almost totally theatre." Carroll O'Connor to JY, January 28, 1975.
43 MacGowran's immoderate drinking... Ibid; Hilton Edwards to JY; Denis Brennan to JY, October 20, 1975.
44 "...the entire future..." Michael-Clarke Laurence to JY.
44 "...to the Beckett wagon." Hilton Edwards to JY.
44 "...French sense, necessarily." Micheál Mac Liammóir to JY, July 10, 1975.
44 "...sensitive actors would respond to." Cyril Cusack to JY, June 20, 1975.
45 ...and Cusack deferred. Carroll O'Connor to JY.
46 ...create a little drama. Siobhán McKenna to JY, Denis Brennan to JY, Gloria MacGowran to JY.
49 "...to his own personality." Siobhán McKenna to JY.
49 "...crowned but for Joan." Denis Brennan to JY.
49 ...they wanted more freedom... Michael O'Herlihy to JY, November 21, 1976; Denis Brennan to JY.
49 ...full-scale rivalry... Denis Brennan to JY, Concepta Fennell to JY.
49 "...mother-ridden country" Melvyn Douglas to JY, March 16, 1979.

CHAPTER 4
50 "very ruthless but..." MacGowran to JY.
50 "...no more drinking." Noel Purcell to JY, July 18, 1975.
51 "...audiences love him." *The Kensington Post*, January 25, 1957.
51 Jack also struck up... Gloria MacGowran to JY; Eileen O'Casey to JY, July 8, 1975.
51 ...end of his days." MacGowran to Hickey and Smith.
52 "...translated into English." MacGowran to Richard Toscan, *Theatre Quarterly*.
53 ...pinned down to a deadline. Martin Esslin, *Mediations*.
53 ...cast them in the play. MacGowran to Hickey and Smith.
53 "...a dimension to the writing." MacGowran to Toscan.
53 Jack was terrified... MacGowran to Hickey and Smith. The first meeting of MacGowran and Beckett has often been erroneously reported as having taken place in a Paris café.
53 ...two dozen glasses. MacGowran to Des Hickey, *The Sunday Independent*, May 31, 1964.
54 "...tones of Dublin." MacGowran to Mel Gussow, January 9, 1973.
54 "...a gaelic lilt." MacGowran to Richard L. Coe, *The Washington Post*, March 14, 1971.
54 Behan, who didn't... Beatrice Behan to JY, July 22, 1975.
56 "a tatty little place..." Donal Donnelly to JY, September 16, 1975.
56 ...something that wasn't right. Gloria MacGowran to JY.
56 ...middle of Westminster Bridge... Ibid.
56 "...as well again, ever." Patrick Magee to JY, June 13, 1975.
57 "...heyday of F.J. McCormick." Kenneth Tynan, *Curtains*.
58 ...during a costume fitting. Michael O'Herlihy to JY.

58 "even worse" Beckett to Alan Schneider, letter, January 11, 1956.
58 "more inhuman" Beckett to Schneider, letter, June 21, 1956.
58 "chess game lost..." Beckett cited by Ruby Cohn, *Just Play*.
58 "no elucidations..." Beckett to Schneider, letter, December 29, 1957.
59 "a poor substitute..." Beckett to Schneider, letter, April 30, 1957.
59 ...Beckett what he wanted. Donald McWhinnie to JY, June 25, 1975.
59 "Sam didn't involve..." Ibid.
59 ...failed the playwright. Irving Wardle, *The Theatres of George Devine*.
59 "too avuncular" MacGowran to Gussow.
59 ...unsatisfied with his performance. Gloria MacGowran to JY; *The Times*, January 27, 1965.
59 "...why he was good." Tony Richardson to JY, December 17, 1976.
59 ...applauded for it by others. *The Times*, October 29, 1958.
60 "...wanton drivel." Alan Dent, cited in *The Theatres of George Devine*.
60 unfit... shocked or offended... Jocelyn Herbert to JY, letter, February 29, 1976.
60 "...the same answers." *Endgame*, p. 5.
60 ...marched out in droves. Gloria MacGowran to JY; *The Evening Standard*, October 29, 1958.
60 "...time to learn it!" Gloria MacGowran to JY.
61 "...through the streets." Donald McWhinnie to JY.

CHAPTER 5
62 During the run of *Endgame*... Gloria MacGowran to JY.
62 ...and he left." Ibid.
62 Jack invited himself... Ibid.
63 ...stolen her passport. Ibid.
63 ...money for his wife. Eileen O'Casey, *Sean*.
63 ...written into his contract... Eileen O'Casey to JY; Michael McAloney to JY.
63 Overburdened with... Carroll O'Connor to JY.
64 One morning during rehearsal... Michael McAloney to JY.
64 "...he didn't feel it." Ibid.
66 "...night after night." Melvyn Douglas to JY.
66 "substance to shadow." *The Washington Daily News*, January 18, 1959.
66 "Mr. Stevens..." Michael McAloney to JY.
66 "You can cut it..." Gloria MacGowran to JY.
67 ...she wanted out. Tom Clancy to JY, January 18, 1975.
67 "...merry and malicious..." *The Boston Record American*, February 5, 1959.
67 "...tenements of O'Casey's Dublin." *Newsweek*, March 23, 1959.
68 "I hate to see..." Gloria MacGowran to JY.
68 ...a new play especially... Ibid.
69 "...he was — collapsed." Patrick Magee to JY.
70 ...in the stage door pub. Gloria MacGowran to JY.
70 "It wasn't very loud..." Elisabeth Welch to JY, June 18, 1975.
70 "the perfect qualities..." *The Irish Times*, October 30, 1959.

70   "The secondary clowns..." Michael Clarke-Laurence to JY.
70   "It's a pity..." Peter O'Toole to JY, September 26, 1975.
71   "They were undergraduates..." MacGowran to Gussow.
71   "...for nine months!" Peter O'Toole to JY.
71   ...their pet goldfish... Ibid; Siobhán McKenna to JY.
72   ...his eyes closed... Peter O'Toole to JY.
72   "...refuse to do it." Gloria MacGowran to JY.
72   ...frustrations by this time. Ibid.

CHAPTER 6
74   MacGowran had a tendency... Gloria MacGowran to JY.
74   "...just let 'em hang." Bill Hogarty to JY, October 21, 1975.
74   ...into the drum. Sean Treacy to JY, June 15, 1975.
75   ...you'll quit now." Michael Clarke-Laurence to JY.
75   For three months... Gloria MacGowran to JY.
75   ...robbed by the police... Mary Lydon to JY, July 14, 1975.
75   "from the awful prose..." Beckett cited by Colin Duckworth, "The Making of Godot," abridged in Ruby Cohn, ed. *Casebook on Waiting for Godot.*
77   ...did no cutting. Donald McWhinnie to JY.
77   "didn't work on television." Ibid.
77   "...almost incomprehensible..." Harold Hobson, *The Sunday Times,* June 8, 1957.
77   ...handle his plays. Gloria MacGowran to JY.
77   ...the playwright's encouragement. Eugène Ionesco to MacGowran, letter, August 11, 1961.
77   ...derived from doing Beckett. MacGowran to JY.
78   "...Ionesco adding on stuff." Ibid.
78   "produced enough pathos..." *The Daily Telegraph,* February 13, 1962.
78   When MacGowran was asked... Gloria MacGowran to JY. Deirdre Bair's account of MacGowran's one-man show is misinformed from beginning to end, in *Samuel Beckett: A Biography,* (New York: Harcourt Brace Jovanovich, 1978), p. 554-556.
78   "...selfish thing on my part." Gloria MacGowran to JY.
80   "...didn't mind being told." Donald McWhinnie to JY.
80   "...deformity and despair." *The Irish Times,* October 8, 1962.
80   "...wasn't happy about it." Gloria MacGowran to JY.
80   "A mime is served..." Ibid.
80   "exactly right" Burgess Meredith to JY, November 18, 1975.
80   "an aberration." John Beary to JY, May 26, 1975.
81   ...abandoned the project. S.E. Gontarski, *The Intent of Undoing in Samuel Beckett's Dramatic Texts.* The holograph of *J.M. Mime* is on deposit at Trinity College, Dublin; Beckett reworked the idea as *Quad* in 1981.
81   ...rights for £17.50. Alec Reid to JY, October 21, 1975. Telefís Éireann unaccountably erased the tape of this program within a year.
81   "...on a special occasion." Tony Richardson to JY.
83   When José Ferrer called... MacGowran to JY.

83   "...got a great nose."   Gloria MacGowran to JY.

83   ...never open for MacGowran.   Ibid.

84   ...distressed him no end.   Ibid.

84   *I'll never move again...*   Burgess Meredith to JY.

84   "...sensitive and introspective."   Ibid.

86   "..good for Jack."   Melanie Carvill to JY.

86   "...the image of Jackie."   Patrick Kirwan to JY, June 13, 1975.   Tara MacGowran made her acting debut at age 12 in a BBC TV series; at 20 she co-starred in the film, *Secret Places* (1985).

CHAPTER 7

87   MacGowran and Beckett talked...   Brendan Smith to JY.

87   ...at Beckett's request.   Gloria MacGowran to JY.   MacGowran disavowed directorial credit to appease Beary when the latter accused him of "stealing" his success (Beary to JY).

87   "...*Happy Days* in drag."   Gloria MacGowran to JY.

87   ...answer was still no.   Ibid; *The Times*, September 4, 1962.   Stoppard's first play, *Rosencrantz and Guildenstern Are Dead* (1966), bore the unmistakable influence of *Waiting for Godot.*

88   "How can you photograph..."   MacGowran to John Unterecker and Kathleen McGrory, *Yeats, Joyce and Beckett.*

88   ...with the actor in mind...   MacGowran to JY; Alan Schneider to JY, January 8, 1975.   Schneider previously asserted that he and Beckett "From the beginning... thought in terms of Chaplin or Zero Mostel for O." ("On Directing *Film*," in Samuel Beckett, *Film*, New York: Grove Press, 1969). Schneider denied having made the statement when questioned by the author, then reiterated it in his autobiography.

88   "...not to be seen."   First draft, on deposit at Washington University, St. Louis, Missouri.

88   ...by then MacGowran was committed...   MacGowran to JY; MacGowran to Unterecker and McGrory.   Schneider alleged that MacGowran had accepted a role in a feature film, which made him unavailable.

88   A few months earlier...   *The Times*, January 27, 1965.

89   ...against his agent's wishes...   Gloria MacGowran to JY.

89   "There was a perfect balance..."   Edward Beckett to JY, June 24, 1975.

90   Beckett, who had intended...   Gloria MacGowran to JY; Alan Schneider to JY; MacGowran to Toscan.

90   "No man is an island..."   MacGowran to JY.

90   "Clov is Hamm's eyes..."   Patrick Magee to JY.

91   "...out of this horrible mess."   Beckett cited by Clancy Sigal, *The Sunday Times*, March 1, 1964.

91   His ear for pronunciation...   Ibid.

91   "I can't sit..."   *Endgame*, p. 10.

91   "Sam doesn't actually..."   Patrick Magee to JY.

91   "I only know..."   Beckett cited by Sigal.

92   "If you are lost..."   MacGowran to Toscan.

92 "...purely literary value." MacGowran to Unterecker and McGrory.
92 ...discuss the show with them. *The Times*, January 27, 1965.
92 "a white-faced clown..." Ibid.
92 "...Hamm's dog whistle." *The Times*, July 10, 1964.
94 ...at the Aldwych Theatre. Magee reprised *Endgame* as part of a Beckett season at the Royal Court in 1976. His final Beckett role consisted of a monologue in *Ill Seen Ill Said*, broadcast on BBC Radio shortly after his death in 1982.
94 "...we almost never did." Patrick Magee to JY.
94 The drama critic... Identity unknown, cited by Gabriel Fallon, *The Evening Press*, July 25, 1964.
95 "Sam Beckett is God..." Reported by Fallon, *The Evening Press*, 1969.
95 "I suppose we directed..." Donald McWhinnie to JY.
95 "An Early Failure..." *The Times*, July 10, 1964.
95 "...the age I've reached." Sean O'Casey, *Blasts and Benedictions: Articles and Stories*, ed. Ronald Ayling (London: Macmillan, 1967). Despite his disdain for Beckett, O'Casey loaned one of his embroidered skull caps for Hamm's costume, for the 1964 *Endgame*.
95 MacGowran wanted to... MacGowran to Gussow.
95 "...piece of theatre." Anthony Page to JY, September 8, 1976.
96 "...to stop working." Ibid.
96 "...the sound of them." MacGowran to Derek Malcolm, *The Guardian*, December 30, 1964.
96 "They understood that..." Alden Whitman, *The New York Times*, October 24, 1969.
96 "...levels will be lost." *The Sunday Times*, December 20, 1964.
97 ...a great admirer. It is no accident that Estragon and Vladimir suggest Laurel and Hardy; Beckett borrowed gags, situations, dialogue, attitudes and personality traits from the team, and fashioned them to his own uses. (Jordan R. Young, *Pratfall*, Vol. 1, No. 5, 1971.)
97 "all life finally lived..." MacGowran to Malcolm.
97 "...no more expectations." Beckett cited by Colin Duckworth.
97 "...twice in an evening." MacGowran to Malcolm.
98 "...what he was going to say." MacGowran to Unterecker and McGrory.
98 ...divided into three sections... MacGowran to Malcolm.
98 MacGowran convinced Beckett... MacGowran to Toscan.
98 ...knew his agony... Gloria MacGowran to JY.

CHAPTER 8
100 "..an established classic." *The Irish Times*, February 25, 1965.
100 "Try and have..." Beckett to MacGowran, letter, March 1, 1965.
100 "Oh, *you're* the actor..." Gloria MacGowran to JY.
100 "...director of that ilk." MacGowran to JY.
100 ...must work together. Roman Polanski to JY, May 9, 1974.
101 "He was a tremendously..." Ibid.

101   "three characters condemned..."   Roman Polanski, *Roman*.

101   To his frustration...   Ibid.

103   ...and character motivation.   Lionel Stander to JY, June 6, 1976; Ivan Butler, *The Cinema of Roman Polanski*.

103   ...improvise their own lines.   Donald Pleasence to JY, March 19, 1977.

103   "...to a few words."   MacGowran to JY.

103   "We were shooting..."   Roman Polanski to JY.

104   Jack wore a wet suit...   Ibid; Gene Gutowski to JY, June 12, 1975.

104   "...go ahead and good luck."   Beckett to MacGowran, letter, September 12, 1965.

104   "...entirely different one."   *Radio Times*, February 18, 1965.

105   He decided that major...   Beckett to MacGowran, letter, September 12, 1965.

106   The author was not sure...   Beckett to MacGowran, letter, December 7, 1965.

106   "I haven't a gleam..."   Beckett to MacGowran, letter, July 4, 1963.

106   ...refined in technique.   S.E. Gontarski, *The Intent of Undoing... Eh Joe* was reworked by Beckett as *Ghost Trio* in 1975.

108   ...credit for directing...   Alan Gibson has been credited by some sources as director, elsewhere as co-director. But according to Gloria MacGowran, Beckett was the sole director of the BBC *Eh Joe*. The playwright also directed a production for German television in 1966.

108   "...tension of *listening*."   *Eh Joe*, in *Cascando and Other Short Dramatic Pieces*, p. 36.

108   During a social evening...   Gene Gutowski to JY.

108   "...to write for him."   Roman Polanski to JY.

111   "...glasses dangle absurdly."   Roman Polanski and Gérard Brach, *The Vampire Killers*, p. 58; collection of Gene Gutowski.

111   "...precious case slide away."   Ibid, p. 65-66.

112   "...nose dripping ice."   Roman Polanski to JY.

112   ...name from the credits.   Ibid; *Variety*, July 7, 1967.

CHAPTER 9

113   ...moment from the picture.   Burgess Meredith to JY.

113   During the final weeks...   Gloria MacGowran to JY; *The Evening Herald*, July 19, 1966.

113   "...lived the part."   Fred O'Donovan to JY, July 22, 1975.

113   The fact that MacGowran...   Gloria MacGowran to JY.

113   ...disloyalty and spite.   Ibid; Peter O'Toole to JY.

114   "One evening I was..."   Siobhán McKenna to JY.

114   ...rushed him to the hospital.   Ibid.

114   O'Toole met with...   *The Irish Times*, August 3, 1966; *The New York Times*, August 3, 1966.

114   With his back turned...   Peter O'Toole to JY; Des Hickey to JY, October 24, 1975.

116   "...the rat's teeth."   Seamus Kelly to JY.

116   By all accounts...   Melanie Carvill to JY; Fred O'Donovan to JY.

116   ...make an anti-war... *The New Yorker*, October 28, 1967.
116   Lester also decided... Ibid.
118   "...plays of Beckett." *Time*, November 17, 1967.
118   "Jack turned me onto Beckett..." John Lennon to JY, May 29, 1975.
118   By the time he had... Des Hickey, *The Irish Independent*, April 1967.
118   ...until it was too late. Gloria MacGowran to JY.
118   "...it made its mark." Burgess Meredith to JY.
119   ...without being asked. MacGowran to JY; Beckett's letters to MacGowran.
      Deirdre Bair's allegation (*Samuel Beckett*, p. 617) that MacGowran made
      "obvious hints" to Beckett about a painting by Jack B. Yeats — and that
      Beckett gave it to MacGowran because he asked for it — is false and
      malicious, as is the preponderance of her biography.
119   "...what Sam wanted him to do." Martin Esslin to JY, March 26, 1987.
119   ...MacGowran announced plans... *The Times*, March 18, 1967.
120   "...very faithfully." Roman Polanski to JY. Polanski's 1961 short, *The Fat
      and the Lean*, depicts a master-servant relationship that suggests Pozzo and
      Lucky; his prize-winning *Mammals* (1962) also has Beckettian overtones.
120   ...weeks ahead of the unit. James Mason to JY, letter, December 6, 1976.
120   "...enormous fun." Ibid.
122   "perhaps the old idea..." Beckett to MacGowran, letter, January 2, 1968.
122   "...faithful to every word." Bud Yorkin to JY, April 10, 1975.
122   Throughout his career... Gloria MacGowran to JY.
122   "...as erudite as himself." Maggie Parker to JY, September 23, 1975.
124   ...great identity of views. Peter Brook to JY, letter, January 10, 1979.
124   "...disconcerting vision." Peter Brook, statement issued with U.S. release
      of film, November 1971.
124   "...So did Jack." Paul Scofield to JY, letter, May 1, 1974.
124   When the script called... Gloria MacGowran to JY.
124   Nor was Shakespeare... Ibid.
125   "...must have intended it." Cyril Cusack to JY.
126   "...as time went on." Gloria MacGowran to JY.

CHAPTER 10
127   Mason had suspected... James Mason to JY.
127   "...if we didn't pay them." Burgess Meredith to JY.
128   "...to those in need." *The New York Times*, October 24, 1969.
128   "...proceed on that basis." Beckett to MacGowran, letter, December 9,
      1969.
128   "...fought it and won." Peter O'Toole to JY.
129   ...less shy and withdrawn... MacGowran to Sandra Schmidt, *The Los
      Angeles Times*, January 23, 1972.
129   "...lust for despair" Sean O'Casey, *Blasts and Benedictions*.
129   "...things going our way." MacGowran to Unterecker and McGrory.
129   "...the contradictions." A. Alvarez, *Samuel Beckett*.
130   "the story of a man's..." MacGowran to Lewis Funke, *The New York Times*,
      December 6, 1970.

130 ...developed a talent... Gloria MacGowran to JY.

132 ...like a stray dog. Rita Darragh and Mamie Hamilton to JY.

132 "...comprehend with his toes." Peter O'Toole to JY.

134 When Jack asked Sam... MacGowran to Toscan.

134 "People find Beckett morose..." MacGowran to JY.

134 "...left pocket of my greatcoat..." *Molloy*, in *Three Novels*, p. 94-95.

134 "...gave away, or swallowed." Ibid, p. 97-98. (Ellipses mine to indicate MacGowran's editing.)

136 ...almost paranoid... Gloria MacGowran to JY.

136 "striving for the ability..." MacGowran to Schmidt.

136 "...greatcoat, and it happened." Gordon Davidson to JY, March 31, 1975.

136 Beckett himself directed... MacGowran to JY.

138 "...be there, to direct." Gloria MacGowran to JY.

138 "...way *that* should go." MacGowran to Unterecker and McGrory.

138 "...whole thing is clear." MacGowran to Gussow.

138 When Jack decided he had... Gloria MacGowran to JY.

138 "Jack was like a brother..." Ibid.

CHAPTER 11

139 "...conviction or fervor." *Le Monde*, July 8, 1970.

139 "...you're done for." *The New York Times*, April 25, 1970.

140 ...after rejecting it four times. Gloria MacGowran to JY.

140 Tom Parkinson threatened... Ibid; correspondence from Robert Lantz files.

140 Worse yet the playwright... Gloria MacGowran to JY.

140 ...disappointed in Quintero's... MacGowran to Gussow.

141 Some minor trimming... Robert Lantz to Maggie Parker, letter, October 21, 1970.

141 "The biggest problem..." Louis Guss to JY, January 22, 1979.

141 "What do you think..." Michael McAloney to JY.

142 ...until the dye wore off. Patrick Kirwan to JY.

142 ...expected *Gandhi* to fail... Malachi MacCourt to Melanie Carvill, February 24, 1973.

143 He dashed up the street... Gloria MacGowran to JY.

143 ...the awestruck students... MacGowran to Funke; MacGowran to Schmidt.

143 "I was directing..." Joseph Papp to JY, May 29, 1975.

143 There was one exception... Robert Lantz to Maggie Parker, letter, October 27, 1970.

144 "I think probably..." Gloria MacGowran to JY.

144 "...relaxed frame of mind." MacGowran to JY.

144 "In the present economic..." Lantz to Parker, letter, November 16, 1970.

145 "...see it, embrace it." *The New York Times*, November 27, 1970.

146 "...actors of our day." *The Nation*, December 7, 1970.

146 "...right there with Beckett." Tom Clancy to JY.

146 Jack himself was not... Gloria MacGowran to JY.

148 ...never admit it to himself. Joseph Papp to JY.

148 "...take the octopus and win." Billie Whitelaw to JY.

CHAPTER 12

149 MacGowran sought constant... Melanie Carvill to JY.

149 "...or a bruise." Joseph Papp to JY.

149 Beckett gave MacGowran the words... Melanie Carvill to JY.

149 "...an honored name." *Malone Dies*, in *Three Novels*, p. 244.

149 "...to be social workers." Lourdes Lane to MacGowran, letter, December 8, 1970.

149 "By speaking to..." Rosette Lamont to J. Stephen Sheppard, Lantz Office, letter, January 18, 1971.

149 ...many more offers... Correspondence from Lantz files.

149 Jack had passed up... Cyril Cusack was hired for the 1963 BBC production when MacGowran turned it down; Magee finally reprised his definitive stage performance when the BBC did a more faithful version in 1972. The MacGowran version, filmed in New York in 1971, was done on speculation for *commercial* TV but was never broadcast.

152 "...absorbed in the work." Siobhán McKenna to JY. McKenna, who died in 1986, played Winnie of *Happy Days* in one segment of her one-woman show, *Here Are Ladies*.

152 ...£7000 in back taxes... Melanie Carvill to JY.

153 ...tour company's receipts. Actor's Equity Assn. and Theatre Now Inc. contracts, Lantz files.

152 When Beckett heard... Gloria MacGowran to JY.

152 ...agent was inundated... Correspondence from Lantz files.

154 "...just aren't there." MacGowran to Funke.

154 "It was more his talent..." Cathy Lynch to JY, letter, November 4, 1976.

154 "I know what Beckett thinks..." MacGowran to JY.

154 "I would listen..." Donald McWhinnie to JY.

155 "...people turn on you." MacGowran to Hickey and Smith.

155 ...passed up Pinter... MacGowran to Tom Shales, *The Washington Post*, Nov. 25, 1971. According to Pinter, "Donald Pleasence was always and absolutely the first choice." (Pinter to JY, letter, February 15, 1979.)

155 ...electroshock treatments... Gloria MacGowran to JY.

155 The day he was scheduled... Melanie Carvill to JY.

156 ...terms with the university. Correspondence from Lantz files.

156 ...tired of O'Casey... Gloria MacGowran to JY.

157 ...not around to say no. Ibid.

157 "I was very upset..." Jules Irving to JY, April 4, 1975.

158 ...hated doing the show. Gloria MacGowran to JY.

158 "...exactly the same." Dan Sullivan to JY, May 9, 1975.

158 "It's the type of disease..." Dr. Daniel Sheehan to JY, December 13, 1978.

159 ...rehearsals for the play. Warner Brothers had guaranteed MacGowran would be free for the January opening of the play on receipt of $2,000 "smart money," and arranged to withhold one of his paychecks. (Correspondence from Lantz files.)

MacGowran in the
Works of Beckett

Date given is date of first performance or broadcast.

Further details will be found in the respective appendices.

1957   **ALL THAT FALL.** BBC Radio, January 13.

1958   **ENDGAME.** Royal Court Theatre, London, October 28.

1959   **EMBERS.** BBC Radio, June 24.

Excerpts from Beckett novels. BBC Radio.

1960   **THE OLD TUNE.** BBC Radio, August 23.

1961   **WAITING FOR GODOT.** BBC TV, June 26.

1962   **END OF DAY.** Gaiety Theatre, Dublin, October 5; New Arts Theatre Club, London, October 16.

1963   **ACT WITHOUT WORDS I.** Telefís Éireann, Dublin, May.

HAPPY DAYS. Theatre Royal, Stratford East, London, December 9.

1964   **ENDGAME.** Studio des Champs-Élysées, Paris, February 17; Aldwych Theatre, London, July 9.

WAITING FOR GODOT. Royal Court Theatre, London, December 30.

1965   **BEGINNING TO END.** BBC TV, February 23; Lantern Theatre, Dublin, September 15.

1966   **BEGINNING TO END.** Telefís Éireann, Dublin.

POEMS BY SAMUEL BECKETT I. BBC Radio, March 9.

EH JOE. BBC TV, July 4.

POEMS BY SAMUEL BECKETT II. BBC Radio, November 24.

MacGOWRAN SPEAKING BECKETT. Claddagh Records.

MacGOWRAN READING BECKETT'S POETRY. Claddagh Records.

1967   IMAGINATION DEAD IMAGINE. BBC Radio, March 18.

1968   BEGINNING TO END. Festival 68, Belfast.

1969   Excerpts from Beckett's work. BBC TV, October 23.

1970   BEGINNING TO END. Théâtre Édouard VII, Paris, April 23.

        JACK MacGOWRAN IN THE WORKS OF SAMUEL BECKETT.
        Public/Newman Theater, New York, November 19.

1971   JACK MacGOWRAN IN THE WORKS OF SAMUEL BECKETT/
        BEGINNING TO END. U.S.-European tour.

        KRAPP'S LAST TAPE. Filmed in New York.

        BEGINNING TO END. KCET TV, Los Angeles, November 4.

1972   JACK MacGOWRAN IN THE WORKS OF SAMUEL BECKETT/
        BEGINNING TO END. U.S.-European tour.

Theatre Chronology

1940   A member of the court in **TRIAL BY JURY**, a peer in **IOLANTHE** and a pirate in **THE PIRATES OF PENZANCE** (all Gilbert and Sullivan). Rathgar and Rathmines Musical Society at the Gaiety Theatre, Dublin.

1941   A member of the chorus in **THE GONDOLIERS** (Gilbert and Sullivan). Rathgar and Rathmines at the Gaiety Theatre.

1942   A member of the chorus in **WALTZES FROM VIENNA**. Rathgar and Rathmines at the Gaiety Theatre.

Miss Priscilla Pointer in **DISASTER AVERTED**. Catholic Boy Scouts at Rathmines Town Hall, Dublin.

1943   Nicholas in **THE STUDENT PRINCE** (Sigmund Romberg), directed by Stanley Illsley. Rathgar and Rathmines at the Gaiety Theatre.

A member of the chorus in **WILD VIOLETS** (Bruno Hardt-Warden). Rathgar and Rathmines at the Gaiety Theatre. †

Cecil in **YOU ARE INVITED** (Brendan Smith), directed by Smith. Premiere Productions at the Peacock Theatre, Dublin.

Various roles in **ABRAHAM LINCOLN** (John Drinkwater), directed by Hilton Edwards. Dublin Gate Theatre.

Tram passenger in "Last Tram to Dalkey" (Micheál Mac Liammóir); in **MASQUERADE** (A Christmas entertainment), directed by Hilton Edwards. Dublin Gate Theatre.

1944   **GASLIGHT** (Patrick Hamilton), directed by Julie Hamilton. Pilgrim Productions at the Peacock Theatre.

HOBSON'S CHOICE (Harold Brighouse), directed by Julie Hamilton. Pilgrim Productions at the Peacock Theatre.

The hero's brother in **ONE MAN'S HEAVEN** (Brendan Smith), directed by Smith. Premiere Productions at the Peacock Theatre.

A member of the chorus in **LILAC TIME** (Schubert). Rathgar and Rathmines at the Gaiety Theatre. †

A member of the chorus in **BITTER SWEET** (Nöel Coward). Rathgar and Rathmines at the Gaiety Theatre. †

Cyril Eaves in **MY NAME IS ANN** (Brendan Smith), directed by Smith. Premiere Productions at the Peacock Theatre.

Mr. MacBride in **BUSMAN'S HONEYMOON** (Dorothy Sayers and M. St. Clare Brune). Insurance Dramatic Society at the Peacock Theatre.

Dermot McMurrough and Hugh O'Donnell in **SAINT LORCAN FOR IRELAND** (an historical pageant). Catholic Boy Scouts at the Olympia Theatre, Dublin.

A Dubliner in **NO MORE CULTURE** (Brendan Smith), directed by Smith. Premiere Productions at the Olympia Theatre.

1945   Uncle Bobbie in **THE MOON IS BLACK** (Eamonn Andrews). Blue-White Productions at the Peacock Theatre.

YOU ARE INVITED (revival). Premiere Productions at the Olympia Theatre.

Multiple roles in **A SPRING COCKTAIL** (Brendan Smith), directed by Smith. Brendan Smith-Jack MacGowran Productions at the Peacock Theatre.

A houseboy in **THE SOLVING OF CHARLIE** (Brendan Smith), directed by Smith. Smith- MacGowran Productions at the Peacock Theatre.

Mr. Pim in **MR. PIM PASSES BY** (A.A. Milne), directed by Brendan Smith. Smith- MacGowran Productions at the Peacock Theatre.

Parson in **WHEN WE ARE MARRIED** (J.B. Priestley), directed by J.J. Henry. Pilgrim Productions at the Peacock Theatre.

1946   Arabella Thomson in **THE NEW MASTER** (H.D. Stratham). Catholic Boy Scouts at Rathmines Town Hall.

Jack in **REHEARSAL** (MacGowran) and **REUNION HAS IT** (MacGowran). The Utopians at the Norwood Tennis Club, Dublin; tour of Irish provinces.

Multiple roles in **KALEIDOSCOPE** (Brendan Smith), directed by Smith. Smith- MacGowran Productions at the Peacock Theatre.

PRIVATE HOTEL (Brendan Smith), directed by Smith. Smith-MacGowran Productions at the Peacock Theatre.

ONE MAN'S HEAVEN (revival). Smith-MacGowran Productions at the Peacock Theatre.

Joxer Daly in JUNO AND THE PAYCOCK (O'Casey), directed by Smith. Smith- MacGowran Productions in Lucan and Ballybriggan, County Dublin.

WHITE CARGO. Stanley Illsley-Leo McCabe Productions in Bray, County Dublin. †

The French officer in WHILE THE SUN SHINES (Terence Rattigan), directed by Stanley Illsley. Illsley-McCabe Productions at the Olympia Theatre.

Parson in WHEN WE ARE MARRIED (J.B. Priestley), directed by Stanley Illsley. Illsley-McCabe Productions at the Olympia Theatre.

Albert Feather in LADIES IN RETIREMENT (Reginald Denham and Edward Percy), directed by MacGowran. Pilgrim Productions at the Peacock Theatre.

A leprechaun in FERNANDÓ AGUS AN DRAGAN (A Christmas pantomime), directed by Frank Dermody. Abbey Theatre, Dublin.

1947   AWAKE AND SING (Clifford Odets), directed by MacGowran. Pilgrim Productions at the Peacock Theatre.

Dr. Richard Mahon in THE DARK ROAD (Elizabeth Connor), directed by Michael J. Dolan. Abbey Theatre.

A neighbor in CASADH AN tSUGÁIN (Douglas Hyde), directed by Tomás Mac Anna. Abbey Theatre.

Darby Sullivan in THE GREAT PACIFICATOR (Sigerson Clifford), directed by Michael J. Dolan. Abbey Theatre.

THE SILVER CORD (Sidney Howard), directed by MacGowran. Pilgrim Productions at the Peacock Theatre.

1948   Cnú in RÉALT DHIARMUDA (A Christmas pantomime), directed by Tomás Mac Anna. Abbey Theatre.

AWAKE AND SING (revival), directed by MacGowran. Pilgrim Productions at the Gaiety Theatre.

THEY GOT WHAT THEY WANTED (Louis D'Alton), directed by MacGowran. Athy Social Club Players at Town Hall, Athy, County Kildare.

THE BIRD NEST (Lennox Robinson), directed by MacGowran. Pilgrim Productions at Marist Hall, Dublin.

MUNGO'S MANSION (Walter Macken), directed by Ria Mooney. Abbey Theatre.

THE RIGHTEOUS ARE BOLD (Frank Carney), directed by MacGowran. Athy Social Club Players at Town Hall, Athy.

William Slattery in **DRAMA AT INISH** (Lennox Robinson), directed by Ria Mooney. Abbey Theatre.

Nicolas in **NA CLOIGÍNÍ** (translated by Maighread Nic Mhaícin from *Le Juif Polonais* by Erckmann-Chatrian), directed by Tomás Mac Anna. Abbey Theatre.

Philly Cullen in **THE PLAYBOY OF THE WESTERN WORLD** (Synge). Abbey Theatre.

Murty in **THE KING OF FRIDAY'S MEN** (Michael J. Molloy), directed by Ria Mooney. Abbey Theatre.

LIGHT FALLING (Teresa Deevy), directed by MacGowran. Abbey Experimental Theatre at the Peacock Theatre.

THE DOVER ROAD (A.A. Milne), directed by MacGowran. Waterford Dramatic Society at the Municipal Theatre, Waterford.

Shaun Kinsella in **THE BARN DANCE** (Arthur Power), directed by MacGowran; and **NICHOLAS FLAMEL** (translated by Seamus O'Sullivan from an unfinished play by Gérard de Nerval), directed by MacGowran. Abbey Experimental Theatre at the Peacock Theatre.

A Russian soldier in **BRIAN AGUS AN CLAIDHEAMH SOLUIS** (A Christmas pantomime), directed by Tomás Mac Anna. Abbey Theatre.

1949   **DRAMA AT INISH** (revival). Abbey Theatre.

BLOOD WEDDING (García Lorca), directed by Eddie Golden;

supervised by MacGowran. Abbey Experimental Theatre at the Peacock Theatre. †

Rab in THE BUGLE AND THE BLOOD (Bryan MacMahon), directed by Ria Mooney. Abbey Theatre.

Various roles at the Comédie Française and the Théâtre de l'Athenée, Paris. Further details unavailable.

A desperado in THE SHEWING UP OF BLANCO POSNET (Shaw), directed by Ria Mooney. Abbey Theatre.

Chauffeur in IN SAND (Jack B. Yeats), directed by MacGowran. Abbey Experimental Theatre at the Peacock Theatre.

THE KING OF FRIDAY'S MEN (revival). Abbey Theatre.

A boy in AN PÓSADH (Douglas Hyde), directed by Tomás Mac Anna. Abbey Theatre.

Pastor in THE LINK (Strindberg), directed by Charles McCarty; and Bravery in WAR, THE MONSTER (Mary O'Neill), directed by Tomás Mac Anna. Abbey Experimental Theatre at the Peacock Theatre.

Fir Chomharsan in BEAN AN MHI-GHRA (translated by Paidragin Ní Neill from *La Malquerida* by Jacinto Benavente), directed by Tomás Mac Anna. Abbey Theatre.

Ailbhe in NIALL AGUS CARMELITA (A Christmas pantomime), directed by Tomás Mac Anna. Abbey Theatre.

1950   LES FOURBERIES DE SCAPIN (translated into Irish from Molière), directed by MacGowran. Taibhdhearch na Gaillimhe, Galway.

Ludog Mac Ludramain in UNA AGUS JIMÍN (A Christmas pantomime), directed by Tomás Mac Anna. Abbey Theatre.

1951   Old Heggarty in THE DIRECTOR (L.A.G. Strong), directed by Hilton Edwards. Dublin Gate Theatre.

Charley in DEATH OF A SALESMAN (Arthur Miller), directed by Hilton Edwards. Dublin Gate Theatre.

An Cumadóir Ceoil in RÉAMONN AGUS NIAMH ÓG (A Christmas pantomime), directed by Tomás Mac Anna. Abbey Theatre at the Queens Theatre, Dublin.

1952   An Giobalachán in **SEATANTA AGUS AN CHÚ** (A Christmas pantomime), directed by Tomás Mac Anna. Abbey Theatre at the Queens Theatre.

1953   Filippo in **AN DUAIS-BHEIDHLÍN** (François Coppéé), directed by Tomás Mac Anna. Abbey Theatre at the Queens Theatre.

EVERYMAN (translated by Dr. Ernest Lothar and M.E. Taflar), directed by Lothar. Capitol Theatre, Dublin.

John Maher in **THE COUNTESS CATHLEEN** (Yeats), directed by Hilton Edwards. Dublin Gate Theatre.

Mr. Cooney in **AN APPLE A DAY** (adapted by Micheál Mac Liammóir from *Dr. Knock* by Jules Romain), directed by Hilton Edwards. Dublin Gate Theatre.

Augustus Moone in **THE STRANGE AND UNNATURAL DEATH OF AUGUSTUS MOONE** (Tomás Mac Anna), directed by Mac Anna. 37 Theatre Club, Dublin.

Dick Harrigan in **HARRIGAN'S GIRL** (Seamus de Faoite), directed by Josephine Albericci. 37 Theatre Club.

Shawn Keogh and Philly Cullen (alternately) in **THE PLAYBOY OF THE WESTERN WORLD** (Synge), directed by MacGowran. Cyril Cusack Productions at the Gaiety Theatre; tour of Irish provinces, including Waterford, Cork, Limerick and Galway.

Nicola in **ARMS AND THE MAN** (Shaw). Cyril Cusack Productions at the Gaiety Theatre; tour of provinces.

The Dauphin in **SAINT JOAN** (Shaw), directed by Hilton Edwards. Dublin Gate Theatre.

1954   **SAINT JOAN** (tour). City Theatre, Limerick; Opera House, Cork; Opera House, Belfast.

Roderigo in **OTHELLO** (Shakespeare), directed by Hilton Edwards. Dublin Gate Theatre at the Olympia Theatre; Opera House, Cork; Opera House, Belfast.

A gunman in **THE SEVENTH STEP** (Padraic Fallon), directed by MacGowran and H.L. Morrow. Dublin Globe Theatre at the Opera House, Cork.

The Young Covey in **THE PLOUGH AND THE STARS** (O'Casey), directed by Gerard Healy. Irish Players at the New Lindsey Theatre Club, London.

1956   **HOME IS THE HERO** (Walter Macken). Theatre Royal, Richmond, Surrey.

THE PLAYBOY OF THE WESTERN WORLD (revival); based on MacGowran's 1953 Dublin production. Cyril Cusack Productions at the First International Theatre Festival, Paris.

Seamus Shields in **THE SHADOW OF A GUNMAN** (O'Casey) and The Pedlar in **THE PADDY PEDLAR** (Michael J. Molloy), directed by John Gibson. Irish Players at the New Lindsey Theatre Club.

1957   **THE SHADOW OF A GUNMAN** (transfer); and **LIGHT FALLING** (Teresa Deevy), directed by MacGowran. Irish Players at the Lyric Theatre, Hammersmith, London.

Amédée in **AMÉDÉE** (Ionesco), directed by Peter Zadek. Arts Theatre, Cambridge.

1958   Harry Hope in **THE ICEMAN COMETH** (O'Neill), directed by Peter Wood. Arts Theatre Club, London; transfered to the Winter Garden.

Clov in **ENDGAME** (Beckett), directed by George Devine; supervised by Beckett. With George Devine, Richard Goolden and Frances Cuka. Design by Jocelyn Herbert. The English Stage Company at the Royal Court Theatre, London.

1959   Joxer Daly in **JUNO** (adapted by Joseph Stein from *Juno and the Paycock* by O'Casey), directed by José Ferrer (replacing Vincent J. Donehue). National Theater, Washington, D.C.; Shubert Theater, Boston; Winter Garden Theatre, New York.

Captain Kelly in **THE ROUGH AND READY LOT** (Alun Owen), directed by Caspar Wrede. Olympia Theatre, Dublin; Lyric Theatre, Hammersmith, London.

Jug Ears in **THE CROOKED MILE** (Peter Wildeblood), directed by Jean Meyer. Opera House, Manchester; Royal Court, Liverpool; Cambridge Theatre, London.

1960   Speed in **THE TWO GENTLEMEN OF VERONA** (Shakespeare), directed by Peter Hall. Shakespeare Memorial Theatre, Stratford-on-Avon.

Old Gobbo in **THE MERCHANT OF VENICE** (Shakespeare), directed by Michael Langham. Stratford.

Christopher Sly in **THE TAMING OF THE SHREW** (Shakespeare), directed by John Barton. Stratford.

Autolycus in **THE WINTER'S TALE** (Shakespeare), directed by Peter Wood. Stratford.

1961   Berenger in **THE KILLER** (Ionesco), directed by John Hale. The Bristol Old Vic Company at the Theatre Royal, Bristol.

The Professor in **THE LESSON** (Ionesco). Outside London. Further details unavailable. ††

1962   Drinkwater in **CAPTAIN BRASSBOUND'S CONVERSION** (Shaw), directed by James Gillhouley. Pembroke Theatre, Croydon, Surrey.

Narrator for **PICTURES IN THE HALLWAY** (adapted by Paul Shyre from the book by O'Casey), directed by Peter Duguid. Mermaid Theatre, London; Gaiety Theatre, Dublin.

END OF DAY (adapted by MacGowran from the works of Beckett), directed by Donald McWhinnie. Design by Sean Kenny. Gaiety Theatre, Dublin; New Arts Theatre Club, London.

1963   **THE COUNTESS CATHLEEN** (Yeats), directed by MacGowran. The Dublin Festival Players at the Paris Festival, Paris.

The Night Clerk in **HUGHIE** (O'Neill) and Davies in **IN THE ZONE** (O'Neill), directed by Fred Sadoff. Theatre Royal, Bath; Duchess Theatre, London.

HAPPY DAYS (Beckett), directed by MacGowran; based on John Beary's 1963 Dublin production. With Marie Kean and O.Z. Whitehead. Theatre Royal, Stratford East, London.

1964   Clov in **ENDGAME** (Beckett), directed by Beckett (credited to Michael Blake). With Patrick Magee, Sydney Bromley and Elvi Hale. Design by Matias. The English Theatre in Paris at the Studio des Champs-Élysées, Paris.

ENDGAME (transfer), directed by Beckett and Donald McWhinnie (credited to McWhinnie). With Patrick Magee, Bryan Pringle and Patsy Bryne. The Royal Shakespeare Company at the Aldwych Theatre, London; Nottingham Playhouse, Nottingham.

Lucky in **WAITING FOR GODOT** (Beckett), directed by Anthony Page; supervised by Beckett. With Nicol Williamson, Alfred Lynch, Paul Curran and Kirk Martin. Design by Timothy O'Brien. The English Stage Company at the Royal Court Theatre, London.

1965 **BEGINNING TO END** (new adaptation by MacGowran from the works of Beckett), directed by Patrick Funge; supervised by Beckett. Design by Liam Miller. Lantern Theatre, Dublin.

1966 Joxer Daly in **JUNO AND THE PAYCOCK** (O'Casey), directed by Denis Carey. Eamonn Andrews Productions at the Gaiety Theatre, Dublin.

1967 Seamus Shields in **THE SHADOW OF A GUNMAN** (O'Casey), directed by MacGowran; and Sammy in **A POUND ON DEMAND** (O'Casey), directed by MacGowran (credited to Abraham David). Mermaid Theatre, London.

1968 **BEGINNING TO END** (revival); based on the 1965 Dublin production. Festival 68, Belfast.

1970 **BEGINNING TO END** (new adaptation by MacGowran from the works of Beckett, with the approval and advice of Beckett), directed by Beckett (uncredited). Théâtre Édouard VII, Paris.

Mohandas K. Gandhi in **GANDHI** (Gurney Campbell), directed by José Quintero. Playhouse Theater, New York.

JACK MacGOWRAN IN THE WORKS OF SAMUEL BECKETT, staged by Joseph Papp; based on Beckett's Paris production of BEGINNING TO END. Design by Ming Cho Lee. The New York Shakespeare Festival at the Public/Newman Theater, New York.

1971 **JACK MacGOWRAN IN THE WORKS OF SAMUEL BECKETT** (tour). Kreeger Theater, Washington, D.C.; Western Conn. State College, Danbury, Conn.; Wellesley College, Mass.; Lenox Arts Centre, Lenox, Mass.; Princeton University, N.J.; University of Hartford, Conn.; University of Connecticut, Storrs; John Carroll University, Cleveland.

BEGINNING TO END (tour). Schiller-Theater Workshop, Berlin; Gaiety Theatre, Dublin.

1972 **JACK MacGOWRAN IN THE WORKS OF SAMUEL BECKETT** (tour). Butler University, Indianapolis; Purdue University, Layfayette, Ind.; Trenton State College, N.J.; Penn State University, University Park, Pa.; Caldwell College, N.J.; Annenberg Center, Philadelphia; Harvard

University, Cambridge, Mass.; Opera House, Waterville, Maine; Dartmouth College, Hanover, N.H.; University of Michigan, Ann Arbor; Mark Taper Forum, Los Angeles; Murray Theater, Chicago.

BEGINNING TO END (tour). Gaiety Theatre, Dublin; Funge Art Center, Gorey, County Wexford.

Davies in **THE CARETAKER** (Pinter), directed by Guy Vaesen. Eamonn Andrews Productions at the Gaiety Theatre, Dublin.

1973   Fluther Good in **THE PLOUGH AND THE STARS** (O'Casey), directed by Dan Sullivan. The Repertory Theater of Lincoln Center at the Vivian Beaumont Theater, New York.

† *MacGowran's participation likely but not certain.*

†† *Date approximate.*

No attempt has been made to list variety shows, poetry readings and fund-raisers.

Films

Date given is date of first release or screening.

1951   Billy Kyle in **NO RESTING PLACE**, directed by Paul Rotha. ABFD.

1952   Feeney in **THE QUIET MAN**, directed by John Ford. Republic.

Patsy McGuire in **THE GENTLE GUNMAN**, directed by Basil Dearden. GFD.

1953   Vernon Crump in **THE TITFIELD THUNDERBOLT**, directed by Charles Crichton. GFD.

1955   Sean in **DUST AND GOLD**, directed by John Guillerman. Eros. *

Sean in **DOUBLE JEOPARDY**, directed by John Guillerman. Eros. *

1956   Campbell in **JACQUELINE**, directed by Roy Baker. Rank.

Toddy in **SAILOR BEWARE!** (U.S. title: **PANIC IN THE PARLOR**), directed by Gordon Parry. Romulus.

Mickey J. in "The Majesty of the Law" episode in **THE RISING OF THE MOON** (Three Leaves of a Shamrock), directed by John Ford. Warner Brothers.

Tommy in **MANUELA** (U.S. title: **STOWAWAY GIRL**), directed by Guy Hamilton. British Lion.

1958   Joe O'Connor in **ROONEY**, directed by George Pollock. Rank.

William Bates in **SHE DIDN'T SAY NO!** (We Are Seven), directed by Cyril Frankel. Associated-British.

1959   Dr. Sampson in **BEHEMOTH, SEA MONSTER** (U.S. title: **THE GIANT BEHEMOTH**), directed by Eugene Lourié. Eros.

Phadrig Oge in **DARBY O'GILL AND THE LITTLE PEOPLE**, directed by Robert Stevenson. Buena Vista.

Market porter in **THE BOY AND THE BRIDGE**, directed by Kevin McClory. Columbia. *

Postman in **BLIND DATE** (U.S. title: **CHANCE MEETING**), directed by Joseph Losey. Paramount.

1962   The frightened villager in **CAPTAIN CLEGG** (U.S. title: **NIGHT CREATURES**), directed by Peter Graham Scott. Hammer-Major.

Night porter in **TWO AND TWO MAKE SIX**, directed by Freddie Francis. British Lion-Bryanston. *

Terence in **MIX ME A PERSON**, directed by Leslie Norman. BLC.

1963   Partridge in **TOM JONES**, directed by Tony Richardson. United Artists.

Furber in **VENGEANCE** (U.S. title: **THE BRAIN**), directed by Freddie Francis. BLC.

Father O'Brien in **THE CEREMONY**, directed by Laurence Harvey. United Artists.

1964   Scaramouche in **CYRANO ET D'ARTAGNAN**, directed by Abel Gance. Cocinor. *

1965   Robinson in **LORD JIM**, directed by Richard Brooks. Columbia.

Archie Cassidy in **YOUNG CASSIDY**, directed by Jack Cardiff (replacing John Ford). Metro-Goldwyn-Mayer.

Petya in **DOCTOR ZHIVAGO**, directed by David Lean. Metro-Goldwyn-Mayer.

1966   Albert in **CUL-DE-SAC** (Blind Alley), directed by Roman Polanski. Compton- Cameo.

1967   Private Juniper in **HOW I WON THE WAR**, directed by Richard Lester. United Artists.

Professor Abronsius in **DANCE OF THE VAMPIRES** (U.S. title: **THE FEARLESS VAMPIRE KILLERS**), directed by Roman Polanski. Metro-Goldwyn-Mayer.

1969   Oscar Collins in **WONDERWALL**, directed by Joe Massot. Cinecenta. *

Nat Kelly in **AGE OF CONSENT**, directed by Michael Powell. Columbia. *

1970   Jacques Cabriolet in **START THE REVOLUTION WITHOUT ME** (Two Times Two), directed by Bud Yorkin. Warner Brothers.

Beach attendant in **A DAY AT THE BEACH**, directed by Simon Hesera. Paramount. **

As Professor Abronsius in Polanski's *Dance of the Vampires,* a role created with
MacGowran in mind.

1971   The Fool in **KING LEAR**, directed by Peter Brook. Athena-Laterna.

        Zimmerman in **THE YIN AND THE YANG OF MR. GO**, directed by
        Burgess Meredith. Cougar Releasing. **

1973   Burke Dennings in **THE EXORCIST**, directed by William Friedkin.
        Warner Brothers.

Miscellany

1952   An inept sailor in a film for the British Navy, title unknown [*educational
        short*]. *

1953   Professor MacGowran in **JACK OF ALL MAIDS**, directed by Tomás
        Mac Anna. Abbey Films [*experimental short*]. *

1956   Alf Barber in **RAIDERS OF THE RIVER**, directed by John Haggarty.
        British Lion [*children's serial*]. *

1964   Clov in **ENDGAME**. Mithras Films [*film record of the Royal Court
        production*]. **

1966   Bert in **THE STABLE DOOR**, directed by Pat Jackson. British Insurance
        Association [*industrial short*]. **

1968   Narrator for **FAITHFUL DEPARTED** [*short subject*]. *

1971   Krapp in **KRAPP'S LAST TAPE**, directed by Alan Schneider [*intended
        for commercial television; not broadcast*]. **

1972   Doyle in **THE WIT AND WORLD OF G. BERNARD SHAW**, directed
        by Harry Rasky. CBC [*documentary film for Canadian TV; cinemas*].

MacGowran does not appear in *The Golden Hawk* (1952), *The Young Lovers* (1954)
or *Gideon of Scotland Yard* (1959), as recorded elsewhere; he was contracted for
but did not appear in *Film* (1965) and *Waterloo* (1971). Extant footage of the actor
was used in the Seán Ó Mórdha documentary, **SAMUEL BECKETT, SILENCE
TO SILENCE** (RTE 1984), made for Irish television.

There are two extant videotape records of the New York stage production, **JACK
MacGOWRAN IN THE WORKS OF SAMUEL BECKETT**. One is on deposit at
the New York Public Library at Lincoln Center; the other at Lenox Arts Centre,
Lenox, Mass. Both were made in 1971.

* *No U.S. theatrical release.*

** *No theatrical release.*

Television

No attempt has been made to list MacGowran's non-dramatic appearances. Produced in London unless otherwise noted.

1955   Sean in **SAILOR OF FORTUNE**. Associated.

1957   Michael Donovan in **THE LAST TROUBADOR**. BBC.

1958   The lost man in **A TIME OF THE SERPENT**. ITV.

         Vince in **NO FLAGS FOR GEEBANG**. ABC.

         Emile in **DINNER WITH THE FAMILY**. Associated.

         The Cockney defendant in **THE VERDICT IS YOURS**. Granada.

1959   Huish in **EBB TIDE**. Associated.

         Captain Kelly in **THE ROUGH AND READY LOT**. BBC.

         The Stranger in **CHRISTMAS JOURNEY**. BBC.

1961   Fluther Good in **THE PLOUGH AND THE STARS**. Granada.

         Vladimir in **WAITING FOR GODOT**, directed by Donald McWhinnie. With Peter Woodthorpe, Felix Felton, Timothy Bateson and Mark Mileham. BBC.

1962   Lennie in **ZERO ONE: DONOVAN'S DISASTER**. BBC.

         ONCE MORE WITH FELIX. ITV. ††

         UNCLE HARRY. ITV. ††

1963   **SPECTRUM: ACT WITHOUT WORDS I**, directed by Jim Fitzgerald. Teleffs Éireann (RTE), Dublin.

         Kelly in **THE STRAIN**. BBC.

         A doctor in **24-HOUR CALL**. Associated.

         THAT WAS THE WEEK THAT WAS. Granada.

1964   Father in **POINT OF DEPARTURE**. BBC-2.

Reader/commentator for **JOYCE'S DUBLIN**. BBC-2. ††

1965   **MONITOR: BEGINNING TO END**, directed by Patrick Garland; supervised by Samuel Beckett. BBC-1.

Jeremiah Hudson in **ESTHER'S ALTAR**. BBC-2.

Albert Brady in **CHARLIE NEVER WARNED US**. ABC.

1966   Brother Michael in **SILENT SONG**. BBC-1.

BEGINNING TO END, directed by Chloe Gibson. RTE, Dublin.

Joe in **EH JOE**, directed by Samuel Beckett (uncredited). With Sian Phillips (voice). BBC-2.

1967   Professor Poole in **THE AVENGERS**: "The Winged Avenger." ABC.

Sister Benedict's father in **SANCTUARY**. Associated.

A gardener in **A FIEND AT MY ELBOW**. RTE, Dublin.

1968   Trinculo in **THE TEMPEST**. BBC-1.

Cheese and Egg in **THERE'S A HOLE IN YOUR DUSTBIN, DELI-LAH**. Granada.

Nobel in **HORIZON: IN THE MATTER OF DR. ALFRED NOBEL**. BBC-2.

Banner in **THE CHAMPIONS**: "Happening. " ITV.

1969   Reader for excerpts from Beckett's work. BBC.

Danny Shea in **PARKIN'S PATCH**: "The Birmingham Con." Yorkshire.

1971   **BEGINNING TO END**, directed by Lewis Freedman. KCET Public TV, Los Angeles; filmed in Trona, California.

1972   Michel Lanier in **BANACEK**: "No Sign of the Cross." Universal/NBC, Los Angeles.

Seamus Shields in **THE SHADOW OF A GUNMAN**. KCET, Los Angeles.

As Joe in Beckett's *Eh Joe* — the only performance MacGowran ever gave to his own satisfaction.

Radio

1950   Various roles in **THE CHILDREN'S HOUR** and other programs. Radio Éireann, Dublin.

1952   Bertrand de Poulengey in **SAINT JOAN**. Radio Éireann.

1955   Reader for **W.B. YEATS: LAST POEMS**. BBC Third Programme.

1956   The Old Sailor in **IN SAND**. BBC Third Programme.

The Pedlar in **THE PADDY PEDLAR**. BBC.

1957   Tommy in **ALL THAT FALL**, directed by Donald McWhinnie. With Mary O'Farrell, J.G. Devlin, Brian O'Higgins, Patrick Magee. BBC Third Programme.

The Young Covey in **THE PLOUGH AND THE STARS**. BBC.

Joxer Daly in **JUNO AND THE PAYCOCK**. BBC.

THE BISHOP'S BONFIRE. BBC.

1958   Mulligan in **THE FROST OF HEAVEN**. BBC.

Father Michaels in **THE OCEAN**. BBC.

Captain Kelly in **THE ROUGH AND READY LOT**. BBC Third Programme.

1959   Henry in **EMBERS**, directed by Donald McWhinnie. With Kathleen Michael, Patrick Magee, Kathleen Helme. BBC Third Programme.

Sganarelle in **DON JUAN**. BBC Third Programme.

Reader for excerpts from Beckett novels, directed by Donald McWhinnie. BBC. ††

1960   Aleel in **THE COUNTESS CATHLEEN**. BBC Third Programme.

THE OLD TUNE (adapted by Beckett from *La Manivelle* by Robert Pinget), produced by Barbara Bray. With Patrick Magee. BBC Third Programme.

1961   The Caller in **THE KNOCKING**. BBC Third Programme.

Giggles Devoy in **ANYBODY HERE SEEN FRIDAY?** BBC Third Programme.

1962   THE MOON IN THE YELLOW RIVER. BBC, Belfast.

Reader for **MY KINGDOM FOR A DRINK: HOMAGE TO JAMES JOYCE.** BBC Third Programme.

STEPHEN D. BBC. ††

1964   Reader for **THE CHERRY ORCHARD.** BBC Third Programme.

1966   Reader for **POEMS BY SAMUEL BECKETT I**, produced by Martin Esslin; supervised by Beckett. BBC Third Programme.

NO FIXED ABODE. BBC.

Reader for **POEMS BY SAMUEL BECKETT II**, produced by Martin Esslin; supervised by Beckett. BBC Third Programme.

1967   Reader for **IMAGINATION DEAD IMAGINE**, produced by Martin Esslin; supervised by Beckett. BBC Third Programme.

Reader for **A BOOK AT BEDTIME: SHERRY FOR THE LORD LIEUTENANT.** BBC.

Records

1956   PLAYBOY OF THE WESTERN WORLD. Based on MacGowran's 1953 production. Columbia.

1959   Joxer in JUNO. The New York production. Columbia.

Jug Ears in THE CROOKED MILE. The London production. Her Master's Voice/EMI CLP 1298.

1961   SHAKESPEARE AT STRATFORD. Argo. †

1966   Lavanche in ALL'S WELL THAT ENDS WELL. Caedmon SRS-M-212.

MacGOWRAN SPEAKING BECKETT, supervised by Beckett. Claddagh CCT-3.

MacGOWRAN READING BECKETT'S POETRY, supervised by Beckett. Claddagh [*no release*]. ††

† *MacGowran's participation likely but not certain.*

†† *Date approximate.*

Bibliography

Anon. "Why Actors are Fascinated by Beckett's Theatre," *The Times*, London, January 27, 1965.

Alvarez, A. *Samuel Beckett*, New York: Viking, 1973.

Blevins, Winfred. "Comedy and Despair," *The Los Angeles Herald-Examiner*, February 13, 1972.

Butler, Ivan. *The Cinema of Roman Polanski*, London: A. Zwemmer, 1970.

Coe, Richard L. "Jack MacGowran's Beckett," *The Washington Post*, March 14, 1971.

Cohn, Ruby, ed. *Casebook on Waiting for Godot*, New York: Grove Press, 1967.

_____. *Just Play: Beckett's Theatre*, Princeton University Press, 1980.

Edwards, Hilton. "The Irish Theatre," in George Freedley and John Reeves, ed. *A History of the Theatre*, New York: Crown, 1968.

Esslin, Martin, *Mediations: Essays on Brecht, Beckett and the Media*, Baton Rouge: Louisiana State University Press, 1980.

Fallon, Gabriel. "Experiments, Beckett and the Other Yeats," *The Evening Press*, Dublin, July 25, 1964.

Fletcher, John and Spurling, John. *Beckett: A Study of His Plays*, New York: Hill and Wang, 1972.

Funke, Lewis. "MacGowran, the Great," *The New York Times*, December 6, 1970.

Gontarski, S.E. *The Intent of Undoing in Samuel Beckett's Dramatic Texts*, Bloomington: Indiana University Press, 1985.

Gussow, Mel. "The Quintessence of Beckett," *The New York Times*, November 20, 1970.

_____. Interview with Jack MacGowran, January 9, 1973; unpublished.

Hickey, Des and Smith, Gus. *A Paler Shade of Green*, London: Frewin, 1972.

Kott, Jan. *Shakespeare Our Contemporary*, London: Methuen, 1964.

Krause, David. *Sean O'Casey: The Man and His Work,* London: MacGibbon and Kee, 1960.

MacGowran, Jack. Preface, in Jack B. Yeats, *In Sand,* Dublin: Dolmen Press, 1964.

_____. "Working with Samuel Beckett," in John Calder, ed. *Beckett at 60: A Festschrift,* London: Calder and Boyars, 1966.

_____. "Jack MacGowran," *Performing Arts,* February 1972.

_____. Autobiographical fragment, circa 1972; unpublished.

Malcolm, Derek. "The Day the Malt Fused," *The Guardian,* December 30, 1964.

McArthur, Colin. "Polanski," *Sight and Sound,* Winter 1968-69.

McCann, Sean, ed. *The Story of the Abbey Theatre,* London: New English Library, 1967.

O'Casey, Eileen. *Sean,* London: Macmillan, 1971.

Ó hAodha, Micheál. *Theatre in Ireland,* Oxford: Blackwell, 1974.

Pine, Richard, ed. *All for Hecuba: The Gate Theatre 1928-1978,* exhibiton catalog, Dublin, 1978.

Polanski, Roman. *Roman,* New York: William Morrow, 1984.

Reid, Alec. *All I Can Manage, More Than I Could: An Approach to the Plays of Samuel Beckett,* Dublin: Dolmen Press, 1968.

Robinson, Lennox. *Ireland's Abbey Theatre: A History, 1899-1951,* Port Washington, N.Y.: Kennekat Press, 1968.

Schmidt, Sandra. "At Home in the Spotlight That Beckett Shuns," *The Los Angeles Times,* January 23, 1972.

Shales, Tom. "Actor's Actor on Acting," *The Washington Post,* November 25, 1971.

Sigal, Clancy. "Is This the Person to Murder Me?" *The Sunday Times,* London, March 1, 1964.

Toscan, Richard. "MacGowran on Beckett," *Theatre Quarterly,* July-September 1973; reprinted in S.E. Gontarski, ed. *On Beckett: Essays and Criticism,* New York: Grove Press, 1986.

Tynan, Kenneth. *Curtains: Selections From the Drama Criticism and Related Writings,* New York: Atheneum, 1961.

Unterecker, John and McGrory, Kathleen, eds. *Yeats, Joyce and Beckett,* Cranbury, N.J.: Associated University Press, 1976.

Wardle, Irving. *The Theatres of George Devine,* London: Jonathan Cape, 1978.

Whitman, Alden. "In the Wilderness for 20 Years," *The New York Times,* October 24, 1969.

Index

_____

_____

_____

Ship to:

Amount enclosed (U.S. funds)	_____
California residents please add 6% tax	_____
Postage: add 1.50 first book, .50 each additional	_____
Total for books	_____
Reel Characters limited hardcover @ $19.95	_____
Reel Characters paperback @ $9.95	_____
Laurel and Hardy limited hardcover @ $34.95	_____
Laurel and Hardy paperback @ $14.95	_____
The Beckett Actor limited hardcover @ $24.95	_____

Qty   Amount

Please send the following books:

Order Form

_____

Also Available From Moonstone Press

LAUREL AND HARDY: THE MAGIC BEHIND THE MOVIES
By Randy Skretvedt. A behind-the-scenes documentary on the making of their classic comedies, with exclusive interviews and rare photographs.

REEL CHARACTERS: GREAT MOVIE CHARACTER ACTORS
By Jordan R. Young. Candid interviews with 12 of the movies' best loved supporting players from Hollywood's Golden Era.